Fisherville, Nanticoke and Selkirk Ontario in Colour Photos, Saving Our History One Photo at a Time

Photography by Barbara Raué
©2021

Series Name: Cruising Ontario

Book 212: Haldimand County Towns

Cover photo: 601 Haldimand Road 12, Fisherville

©2021 All the photos in this book have been taken with my cameras. I own the rights to them.

Series Name: Cruising Ontario
Saving Our History One Photo at a Time
in colour photos

Books Available in Alphabetical Order:
Aberfoyle, Acton, Ajax, Alton, Amherstburg, Ancaster, Arthur, Auburn, Aylmer, Ayr, Beaver Valley, Belgrave, Belleville, Bloomingdale, Blyth, Brantford, Brockville, Burford, Burlington, Caledon, Caledonia, Cambridge, Carlow, Chatsworth, Clifford, Collingwood, Conestogo, Delhi, Dorchester to Aylmer, Drayton, Drumbo, Dundas, Dunlop, Eden Mills, Elmira, Elora, Erin, Essex, Fergus, Goderich, Grimsby, Guelph, Hagersville, Hamilton, Hanover, Harriston, Hespeler, Jarvis, Kingston, Kingsville, Kitchener, Lake Superior, Lincoln, Linwood, Listowel, London, Lucknow, Merrickville, Mono, Mount Forest, Mount Pleasant, Neustadt, New Hamburg, Newboro, Newport, Niagara-on-the-Lake, Niagara Falls, North Bay, Oakville, Onondaga, Orangeville, Orillia, Oshawa, Owen Sound, Palmerston, Paris, Pelham, Perth, Peterborough, Petrolia, Pickering, Port Colborne, Port Elgin, Portland, Preston, Rockwood, Sarnia, Sault Ste. Marie, Seaforth, Sheffield, Shelburne, Simcoe, Smiths Falls, Smithville, Southampton, St. Catharines, St. George, St. Jacobs, St. Marys, St. Thomas, Stoney Creek, Stratford, Thamesford, Thunder Bay, Tillsonburg, Toronto, Waterdown, Waterford, Waterloo, Welland, Wellesley, West Flamborough, Westport, Whitby, Windsor, Wingham, Woodstock

Book 210: North Bay
Book 211: Fort Erie
Book 212-215: Haldimand
    County

Table of Contents

Fisherville	Page 6
Rainham Centre	Page 33
Nanticoke	Page 36
Cheapside	Page 42
Selkirk	Page 45

    Haldimand County is a municipality on the Niagara Peninsula in Southern Ontario, on the north shore of Lake Erie, and on the Grand River. Haldimand was first created as a county in 1800, from a portion of Norfolk. It was named after the governor of the Province of Quebec Sir Frederick Haldimand. From 1974 to 2000, Haldimand County and Norfolk County were merged to form the Regional Municipality of Haldimand-Norfolk.

    The population centers in Haldimand are Caledonia, Dunnville, Hagersville, Jarvis and Cayuga. Most of Haldimand is agricultural land, although some heavy industry, including the Nanticoke Generating Station, is located here. Some of the smaller communities within the municipality are Byng, Canborough, Canfield, Cheapside, Fisherville, Kohler, Lowbanks, Nanticoke, Rainham Centre, Selkirk, South Cayuga, Sweets Corners, and York.

Township of Rainham

    The first white inhabitants of Rainham were Jacob Hoover with his sons Abraham, David, Benjamin and Daniel who came from Pennsylvania in 1791, traveling in wagons in which they carried all their moveable possessions.

They purchased about 2,500 acres of land from the government. The Hoovers were Mennonites of Swiss descent. The Hoovers were a thrifty and industrious family and soon had large clearings. They became wealthy as they were the first settlers who had any surplus produce to sell to others who came a few years later.

Manufactured items were very expensive so the settlers made as many items as they could. Many of them made their own harness of basswood bark boiled in lye which was a fair substitute for leather.

The township covers about 25,000 acres with stiff clay soil that is very productive and well cultivated. Fisherville and Rainham Centre are the only villages wholly in the township. Fisherville is the center of the German settlement and has a population of about one hundred and fifty people.

Nanticoke

Nanticoke is located on the western border of Haldimand County. Nanticoke is located directly across Lake Erie from the United States city of Erie, Pennsylvania. Unlike the majority of Haldimand or Norfolk County, Nanticoke is a highly industrialized community. This community is southeast of Simcoe in neighboring Norfolk County and south of Brantford. Nanticoke's residential area is bordered on the west by the Nanticoke Industrial Park, home to the U.S. Steel Canada Lake Erie Works and a number of smaller businesses.

The Esso Refinery Nanticoke is on the northeast, and the Nanticoke Generating Station is on the southeast. Nanticoke used to be a bustling farming and fishing community inhabited since the late eighteenth century. Nanticoke adapted to the Industrial Revolution and became a desired spot for heavy industry.

In 1974, Nanticoke was incorporated as a city within the Regional Municipality of Haldimand-Norfolk through the amalgamation of the towns of Port Dover and Waterford, the village of Jarvis, and parts of the townships of Rainham, Townsend, Walpole and Woodhouse. In 2001, the town and all other municipalities within the region were dissolved and the region was divided into two single tier municipalities with city-status but called counties. What was the city of Nanticoke is now split between Haldimand County and Norfolk County. Wind Turbines were installed in November 2013.

Cheapside

Cheapside is located in the Regional Municipality of Haldimand-Norfolk and is part of the City of Nanticoke. In 1854 David Silverthom settled here and opened the first store. He was bought out in 1860 by William Pugsley who called the place Cheap Corner. When the post office opened around 1865 the postal department proposed the present name which was accepted by residents.

Selkirk

Lake Erie shoreline, quiet roads and countryside make Selkirk a haven for travelers. Selkirk is located forty-five kilometers southwest of Hamilton and a short drive from Dunnville, Cayuga, Port Dover and Simcoe. Selkirk is the oldest village in Walpole Township. Settled by the Hoover family around 1800, the village was the site of a mill and an important center for the local farming community. When the post office opened in 1831 the village was called Walpole. In 1855, the village was renamed Selkirk, in honor of Thomas Douglas, Lord Selkirk, who once owned land in the area.

Fisherville

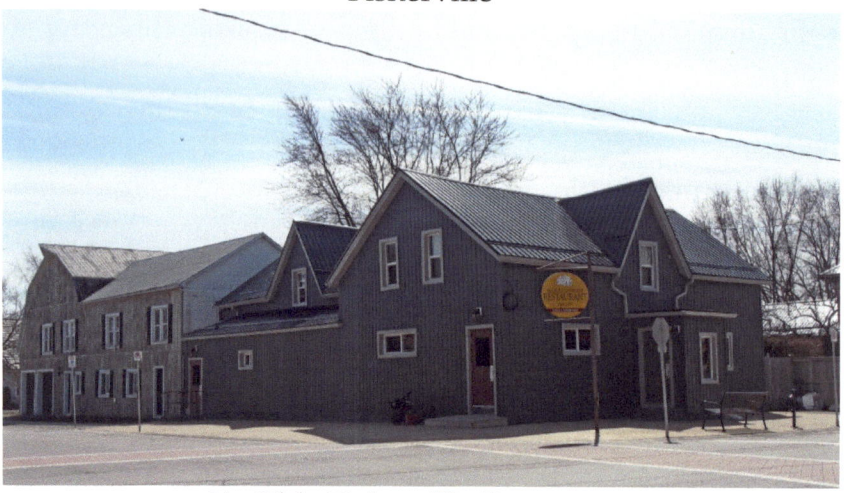

Ye Olde Fisherville Restaurant

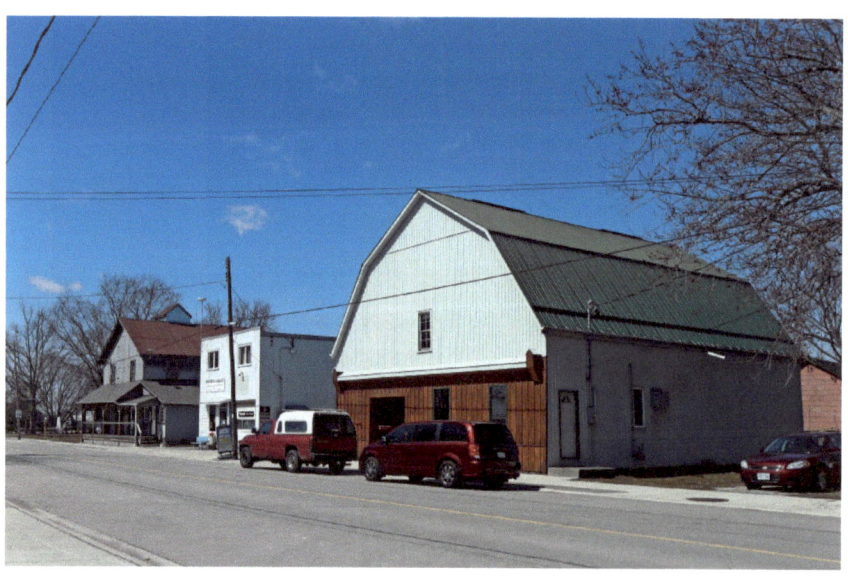

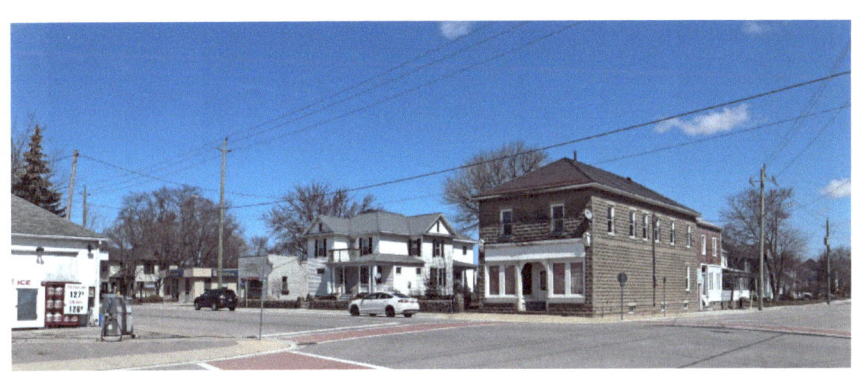

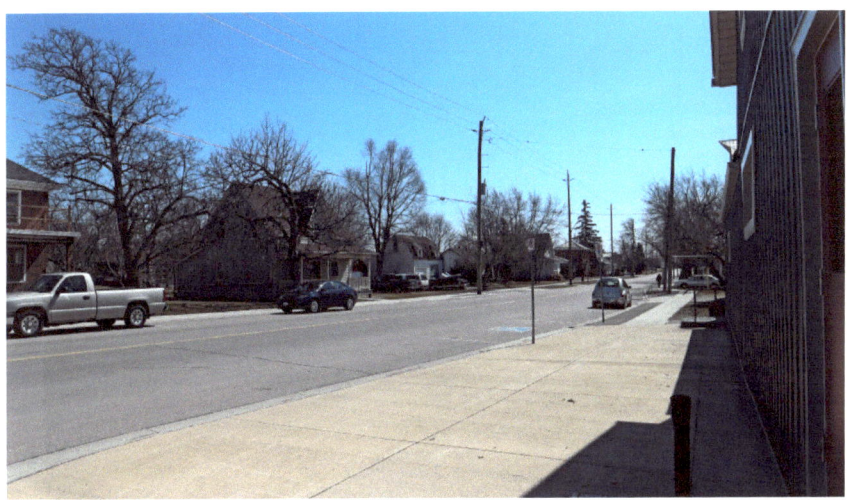

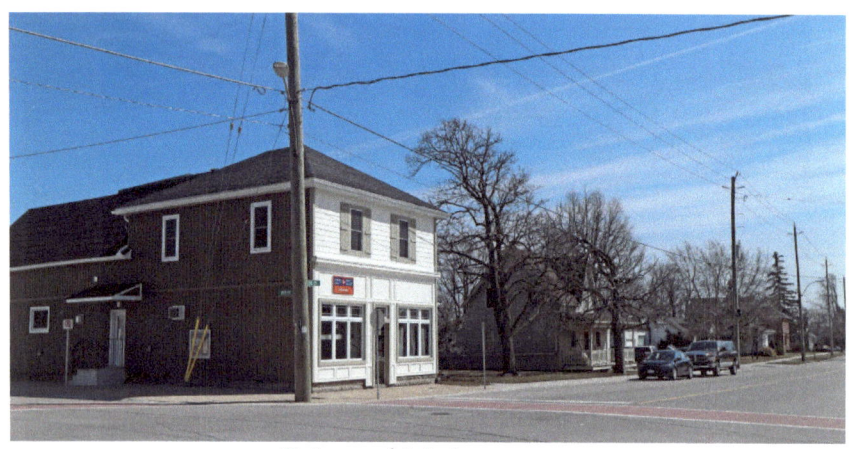
Erie and Main corner

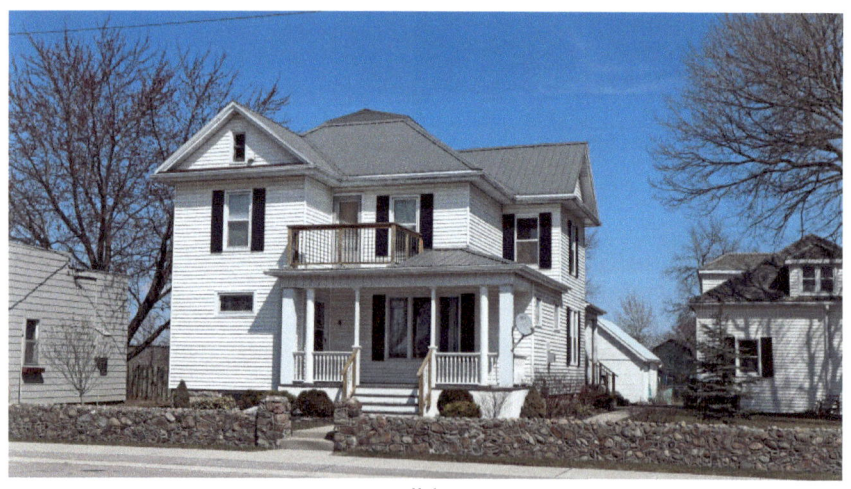
#4

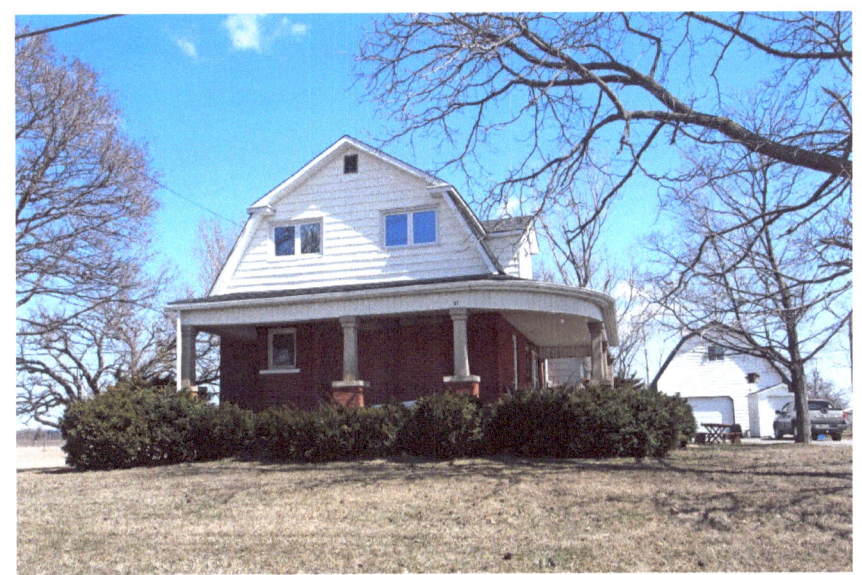

#37

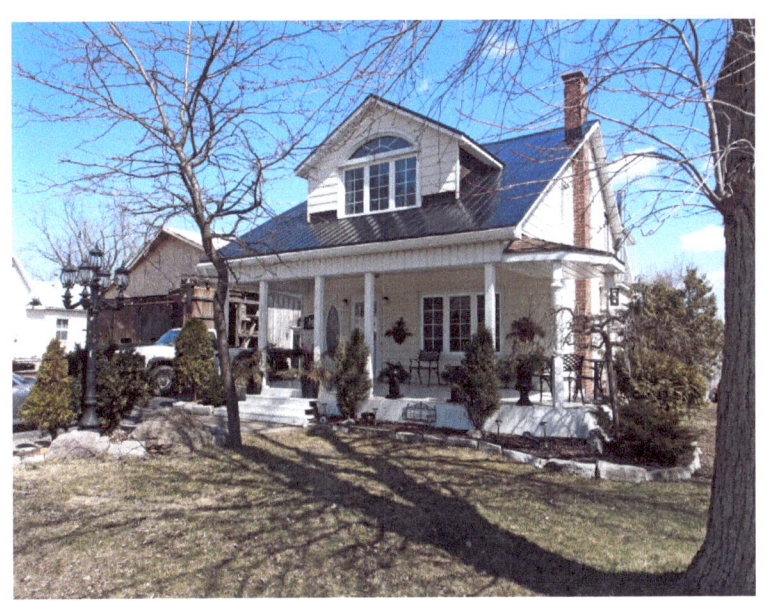

#19

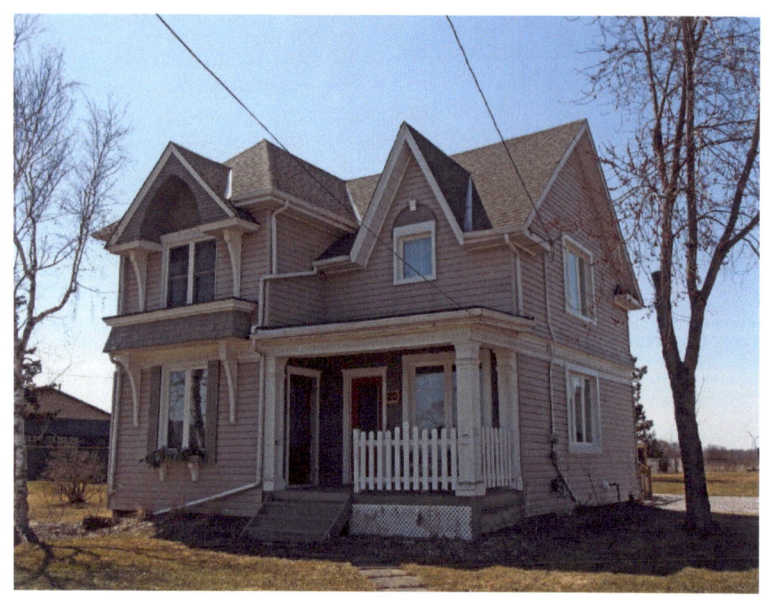

#20

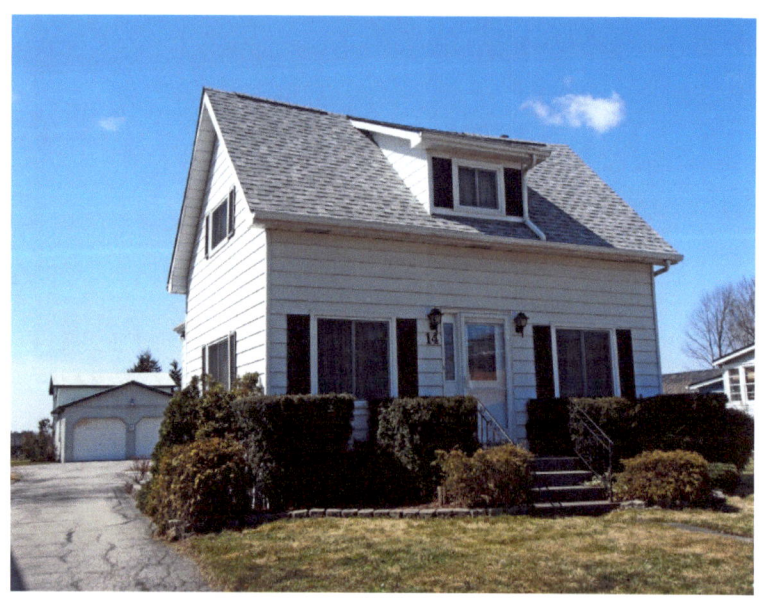

#14

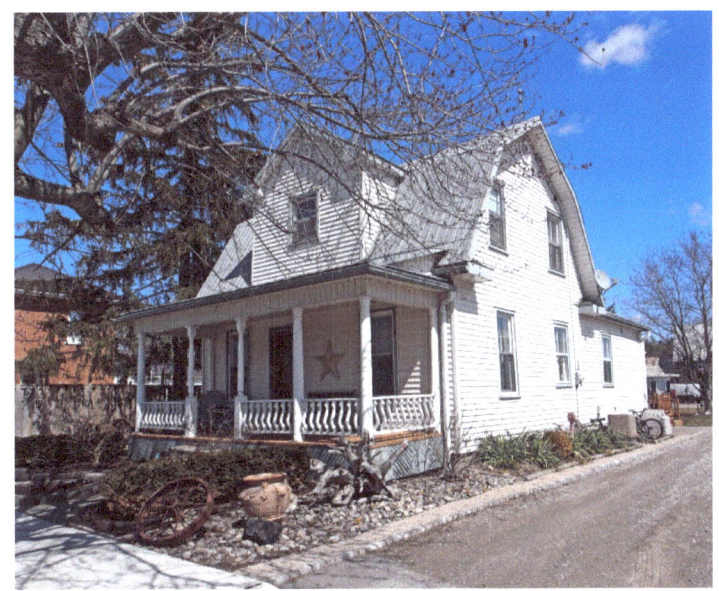

Gambrel roof

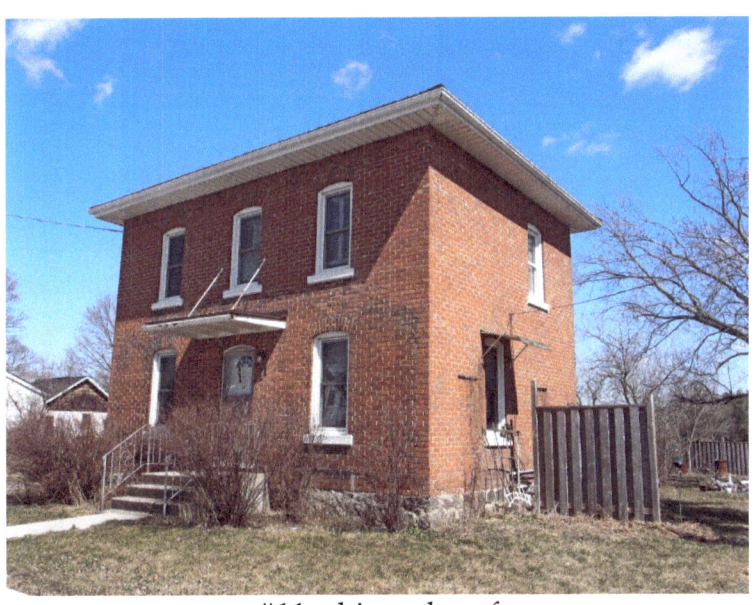

#11 – hipped roof

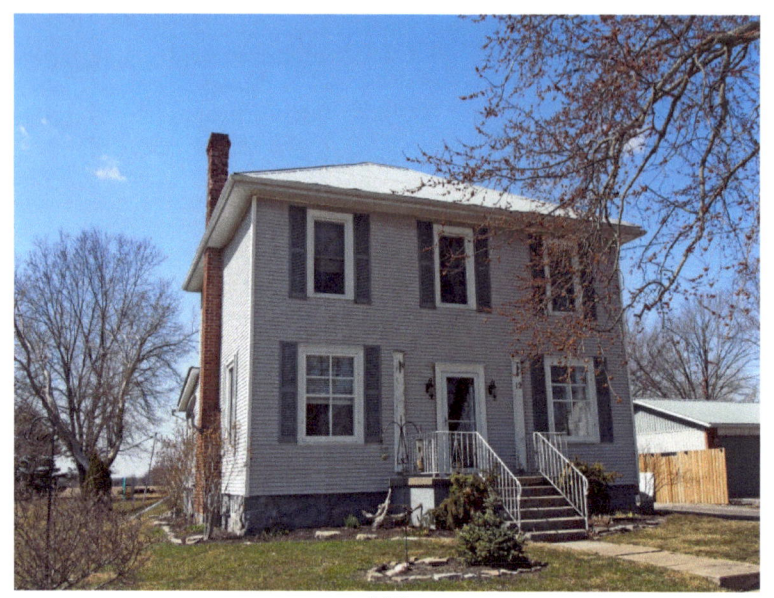

#12

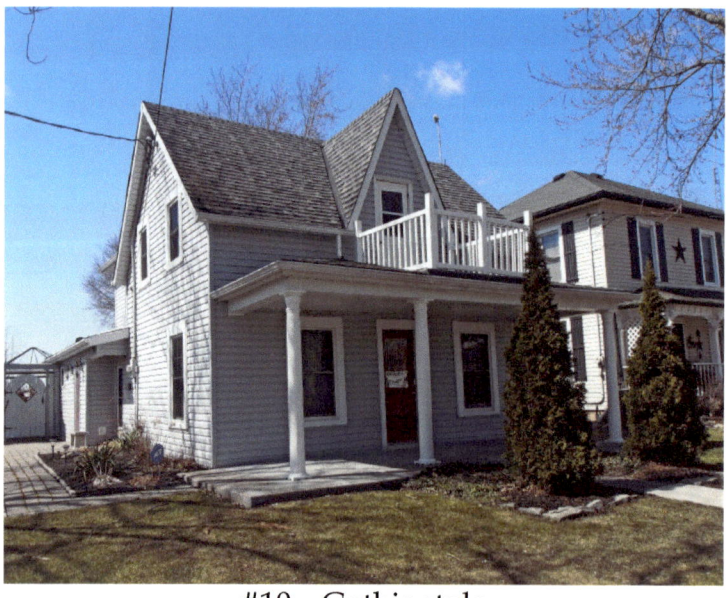

#10 – Gothic style

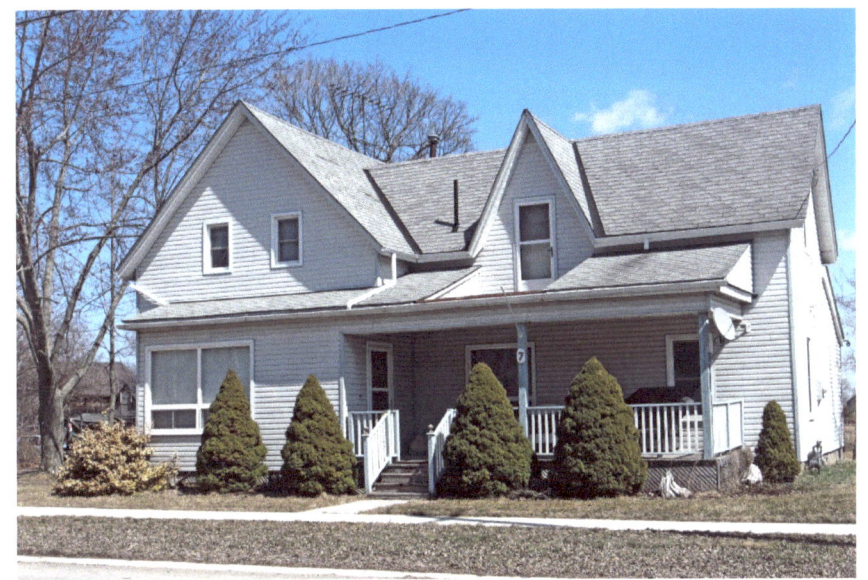

#7

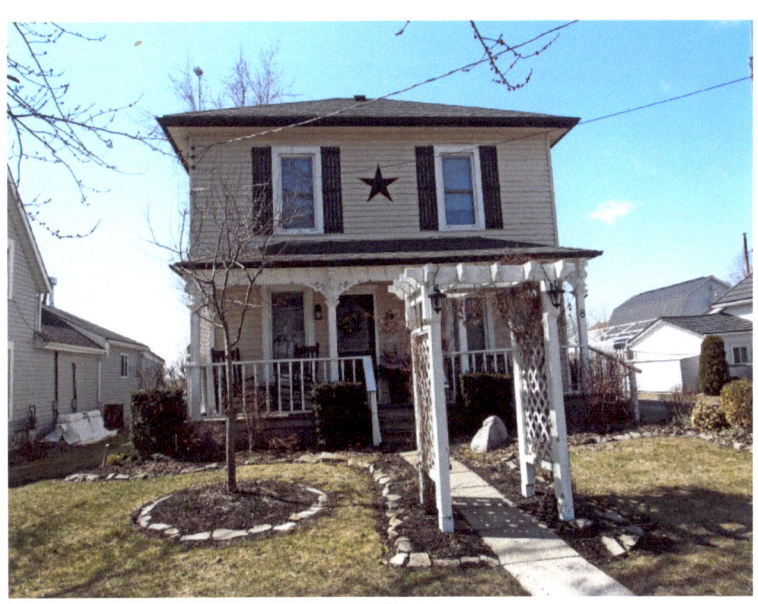

#8

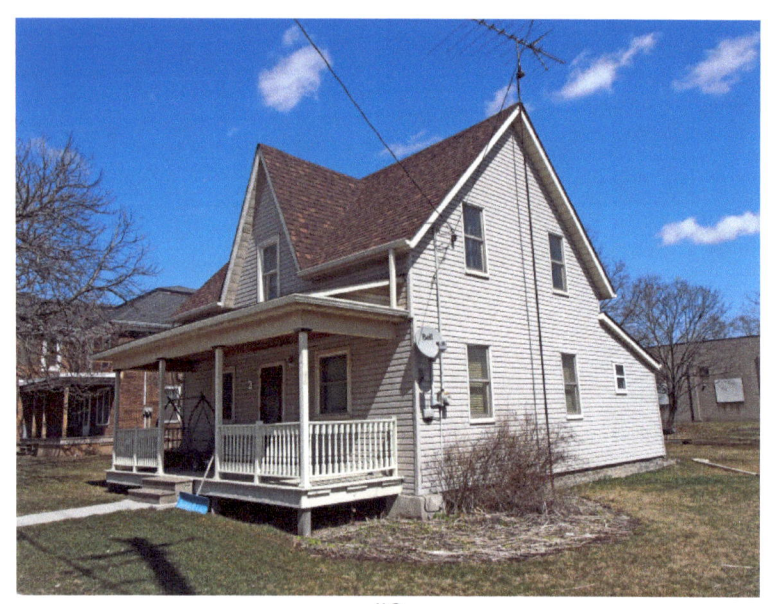

#3

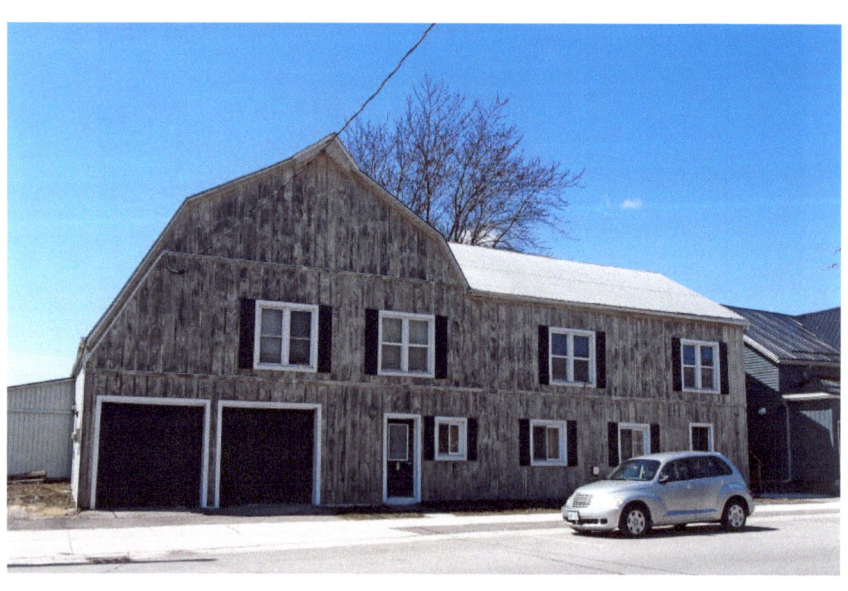

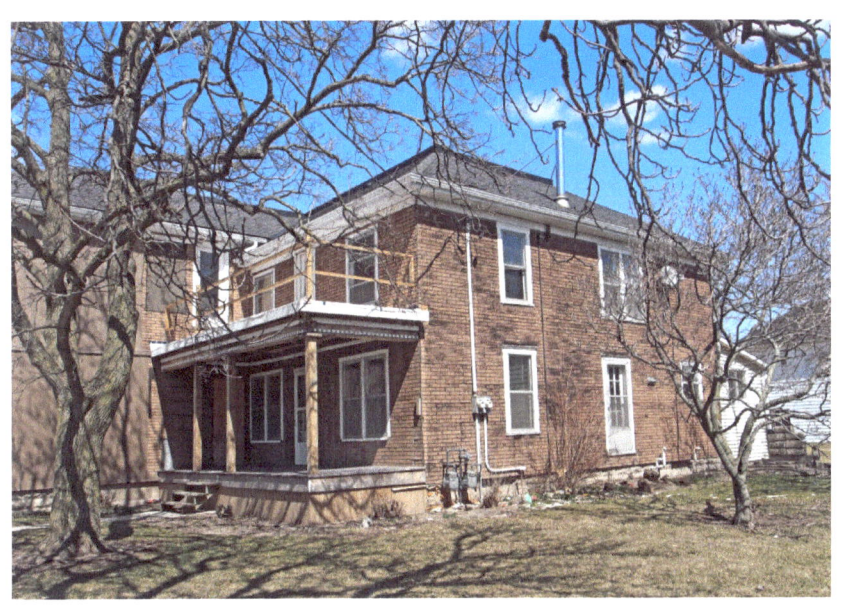

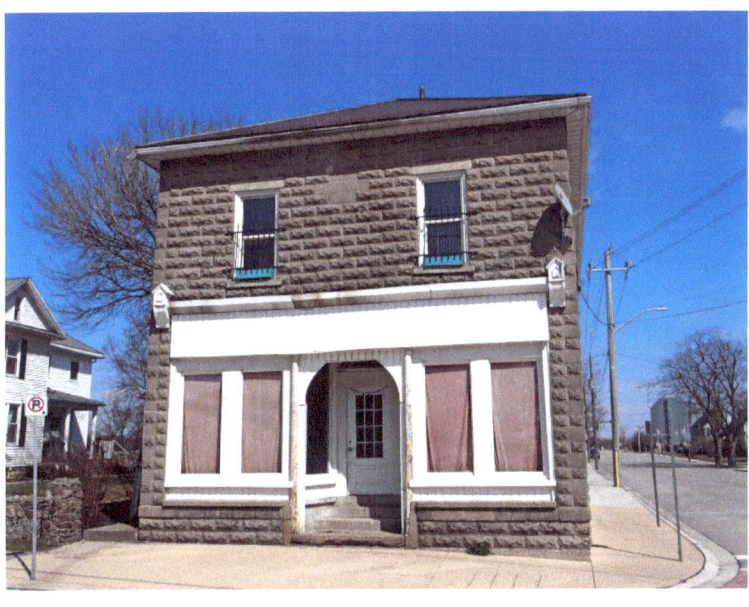

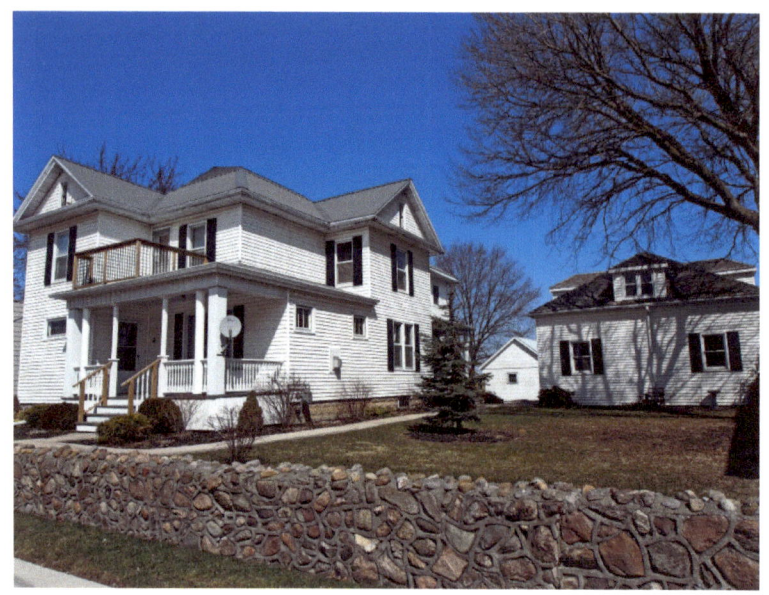

#4

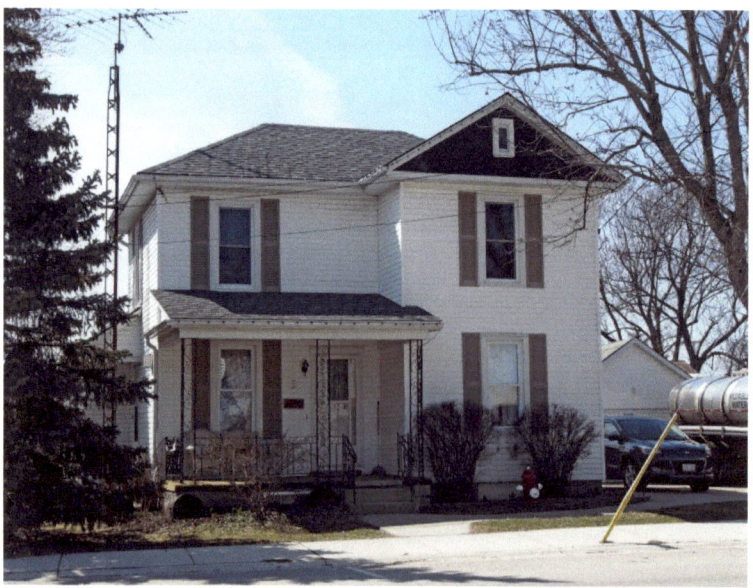

#5

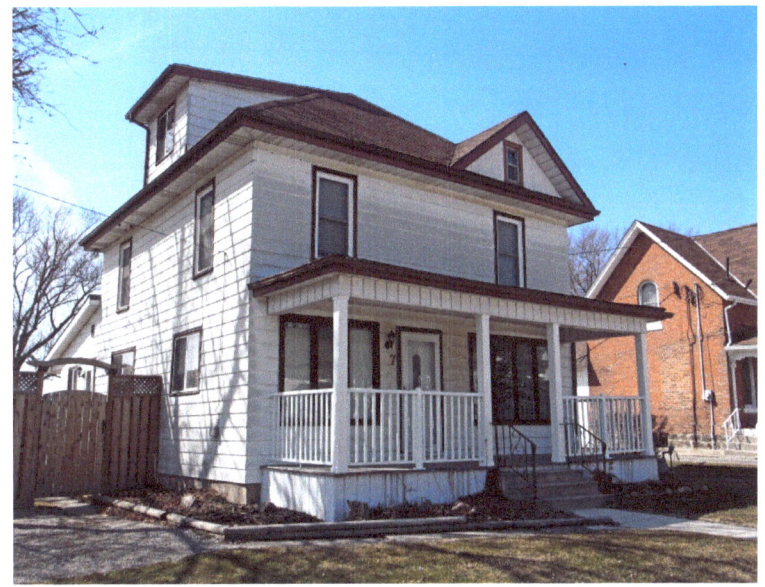

#7

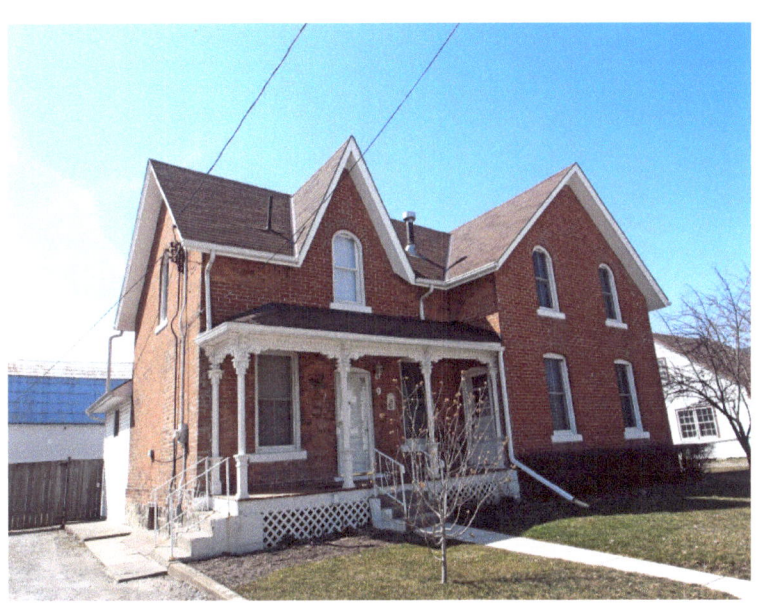

#9

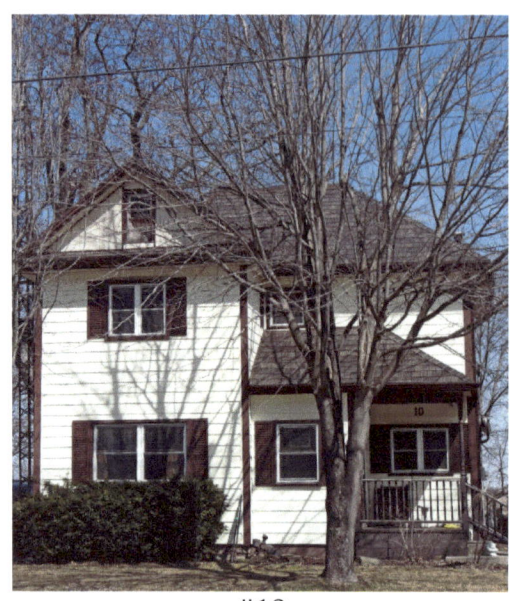
#10

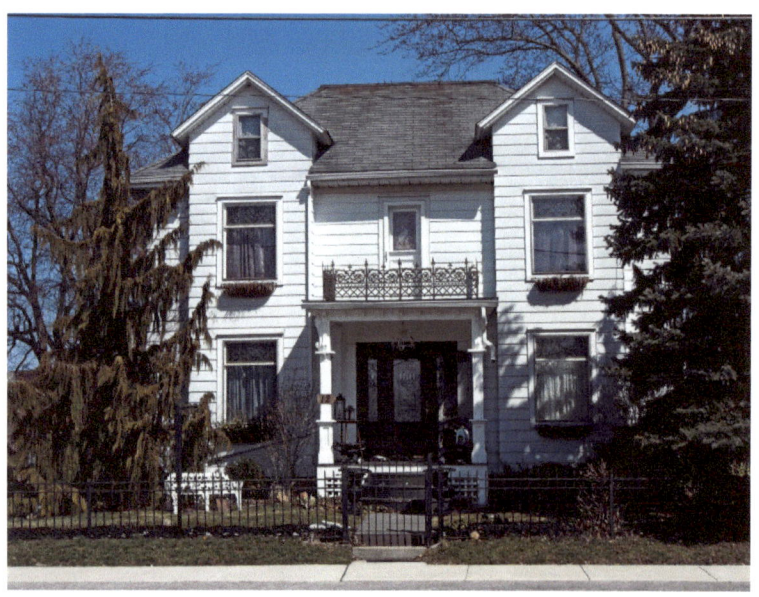
#12

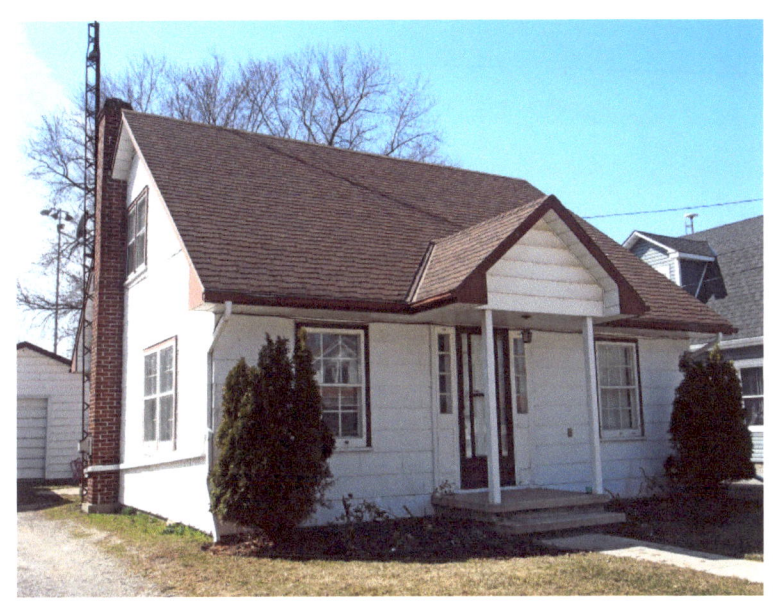

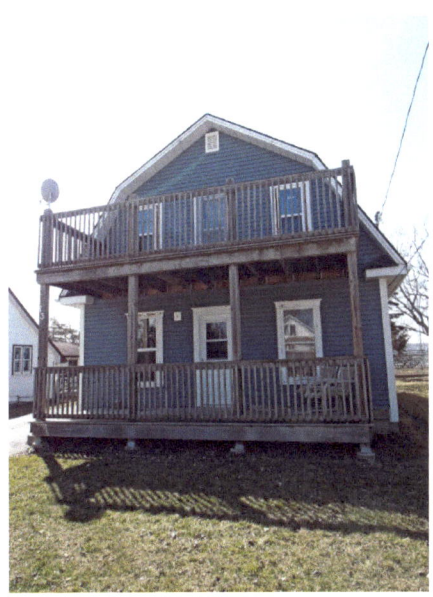

#13 – gambrel roof

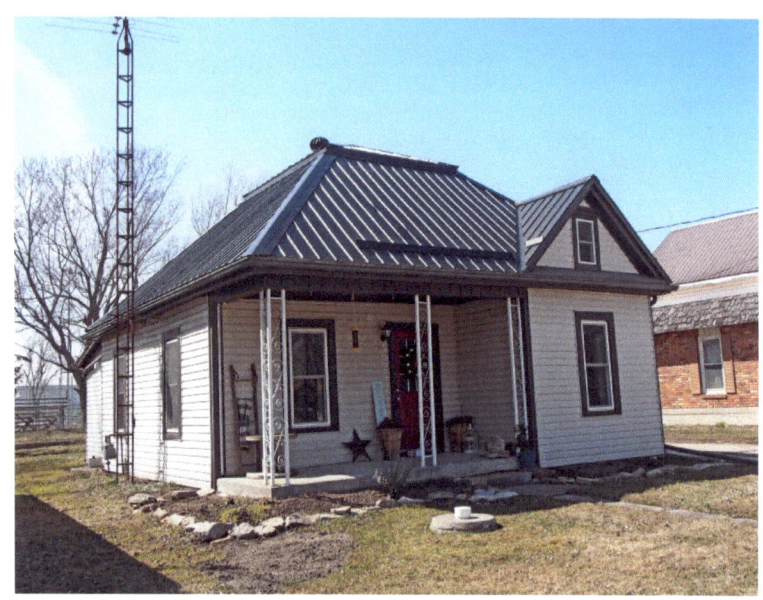

#15

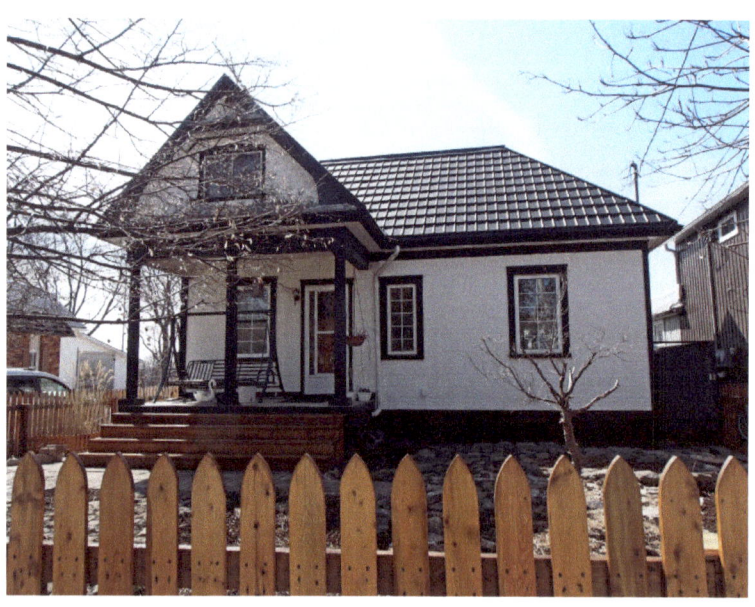

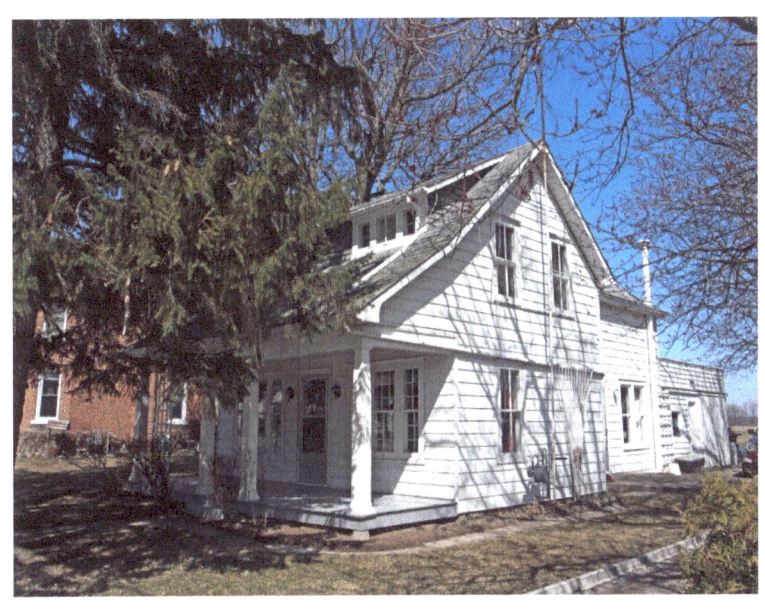

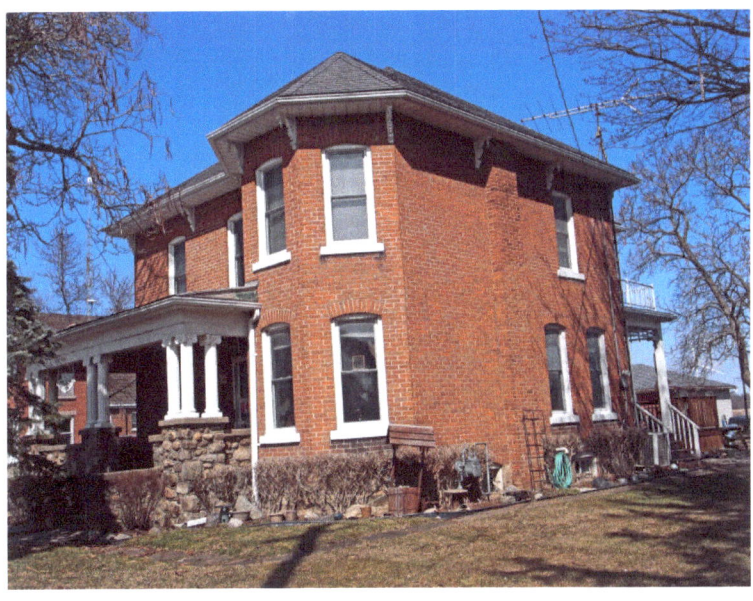

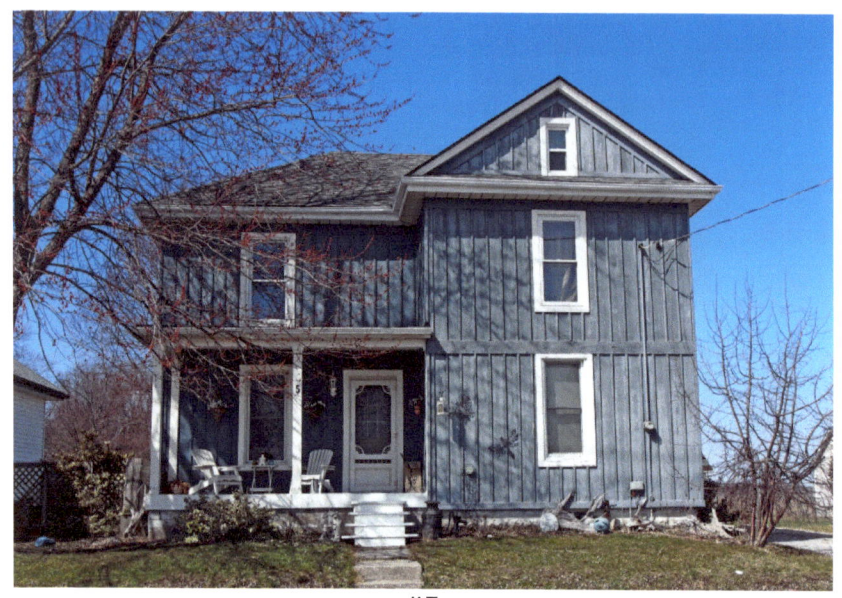

#5

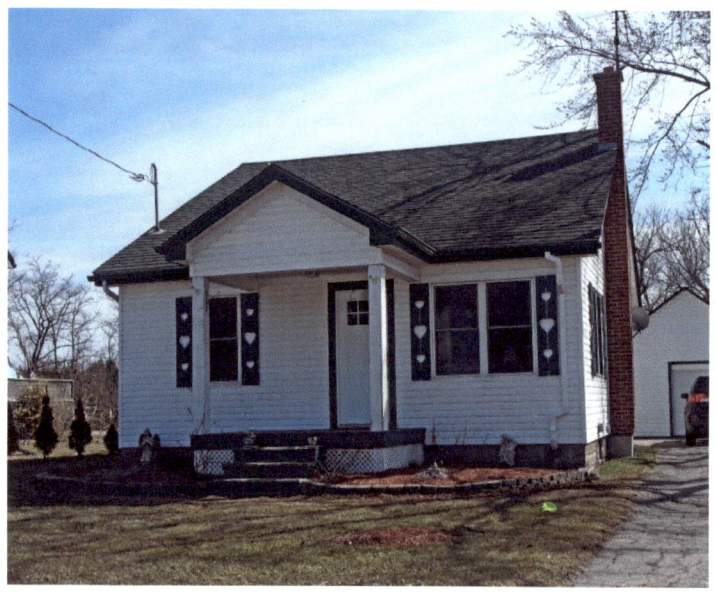

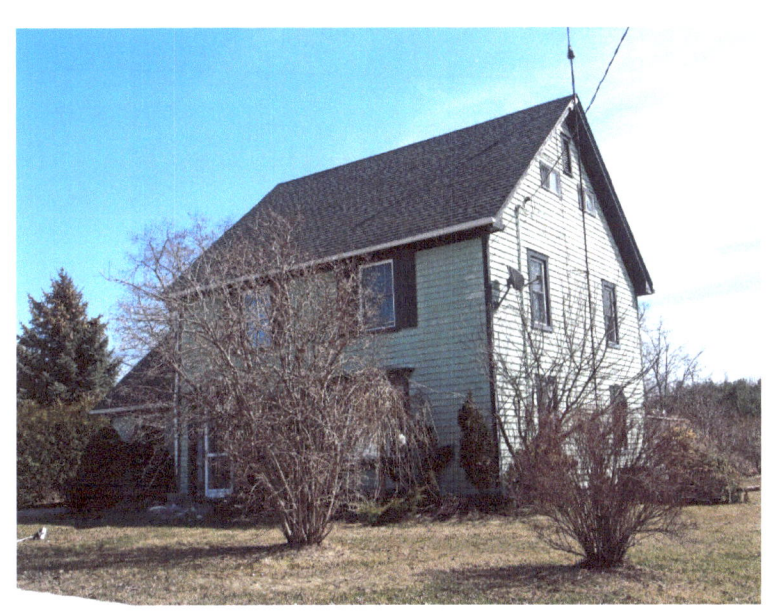

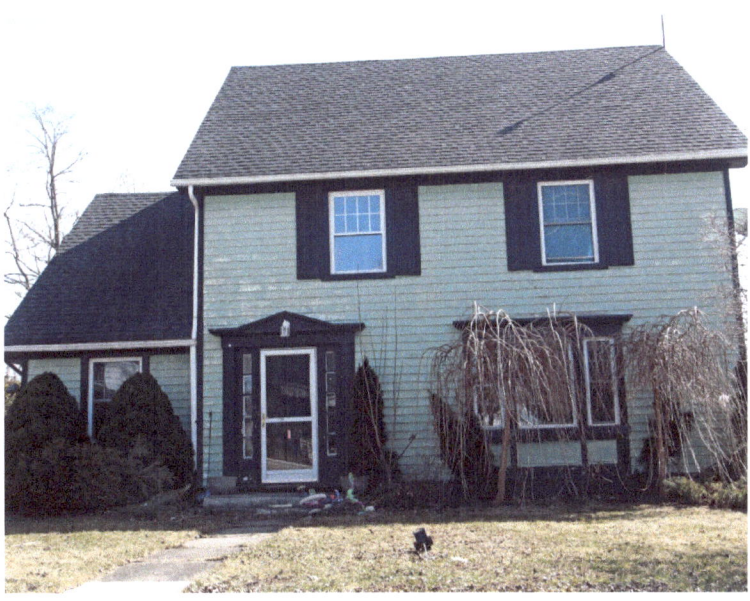

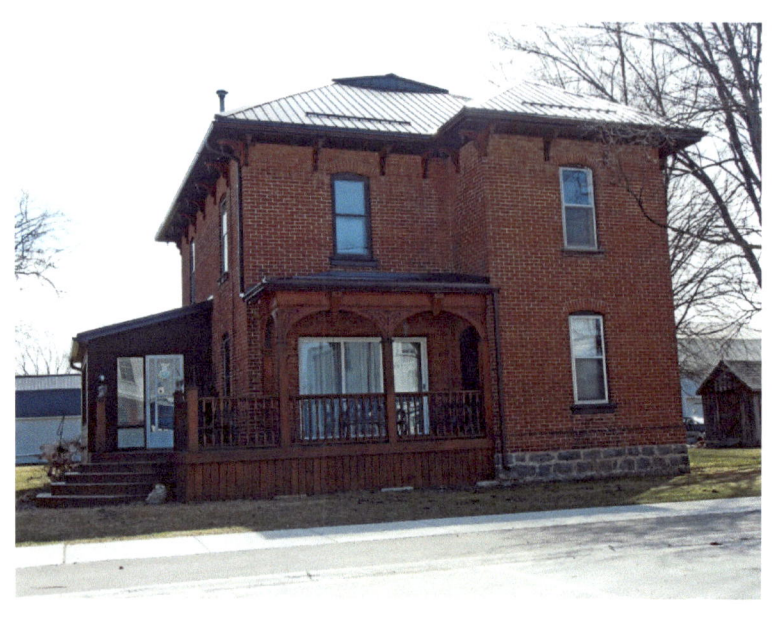

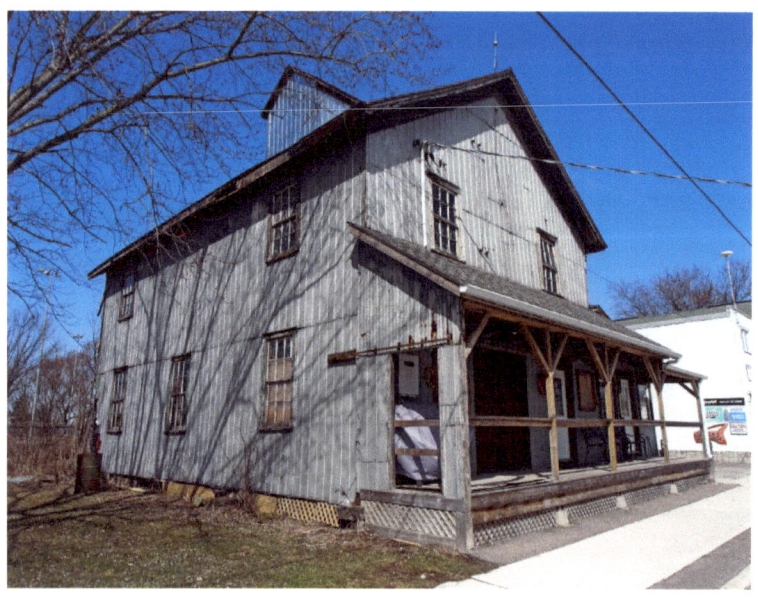

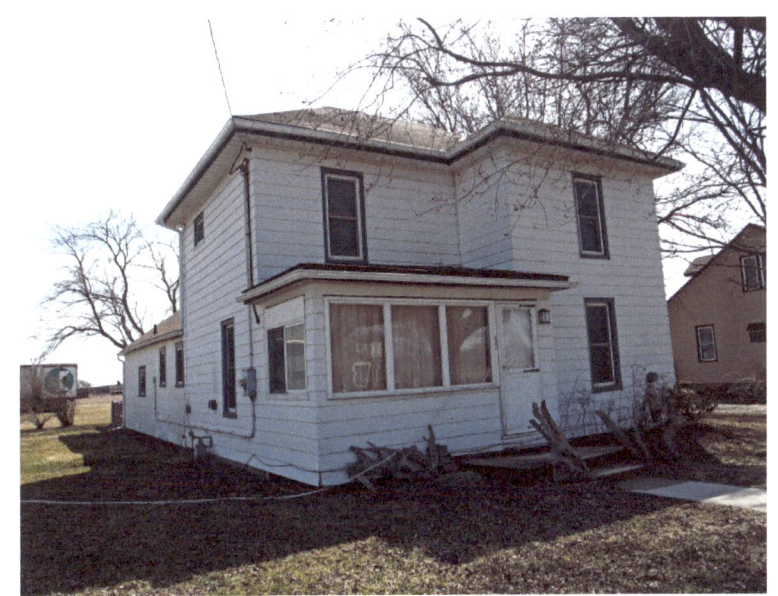

#13

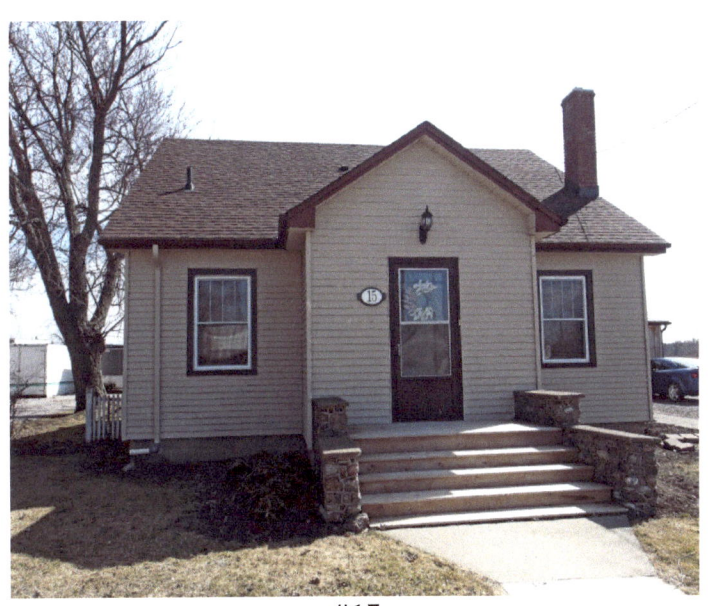

#15

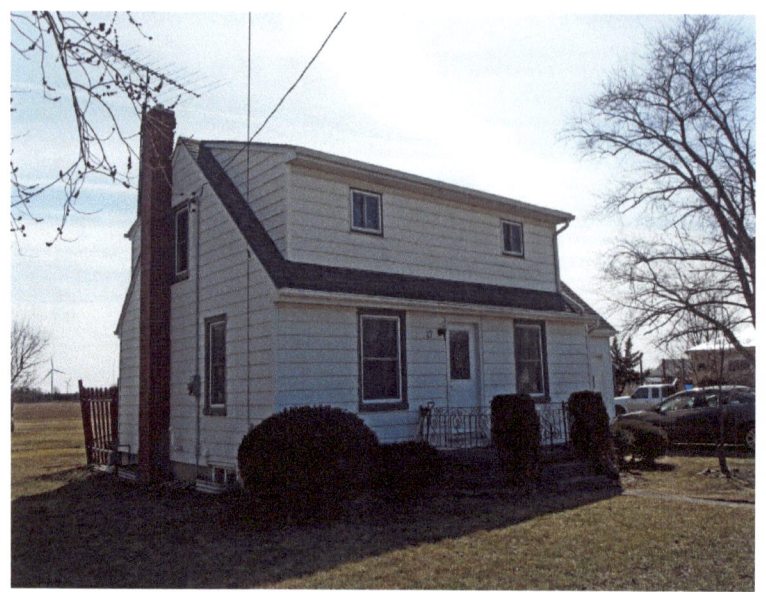

#17

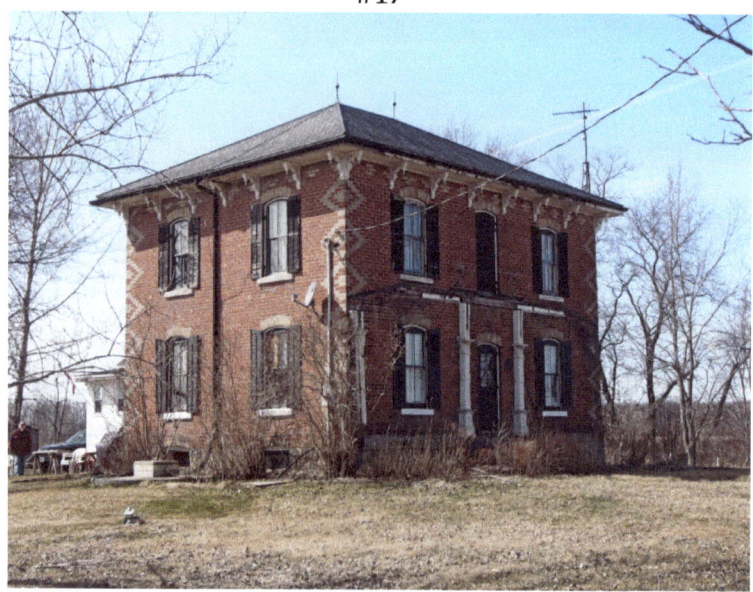

601 Haldimand Road 12 – The Charles Reicheld House crafted by traditional German carpenter Valentine Hartwick in 1886 – farmhouse with cornice brackets, dichromatic brickwork, hipped roof

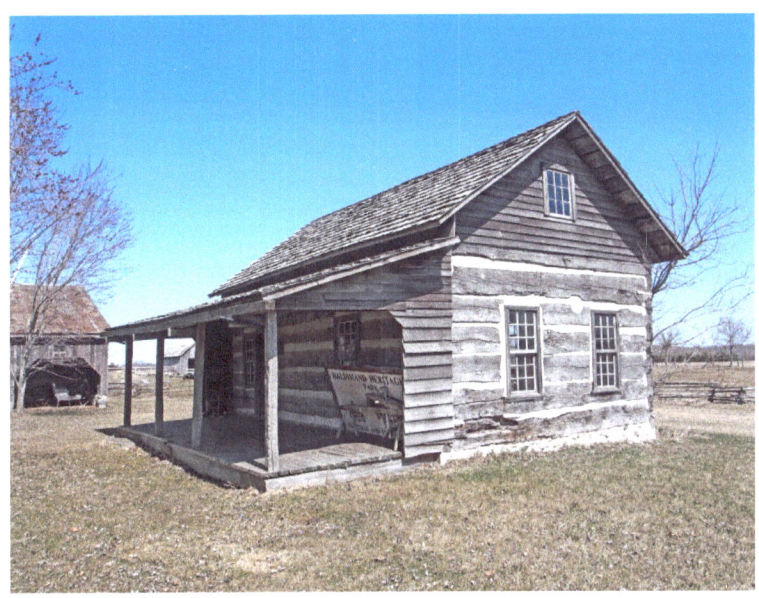

95 Concession 4 – The Hoover log house built in 1793 on the Lake Erie shore south of Selkirk for Daniel Hoover, son of Jacob Hoover from Pennsylvania. In 1997, the fire damaged remnants were brought by Mr. Bill Fletcher, reassembled and relocated on his farm.

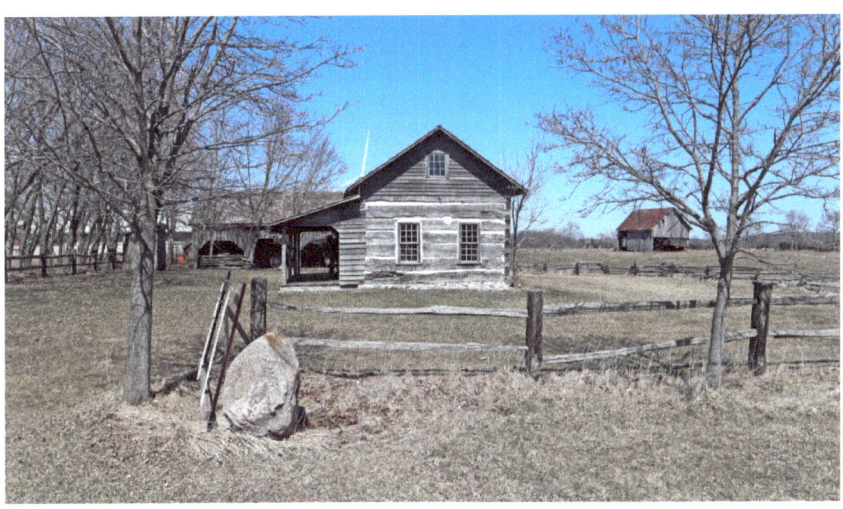

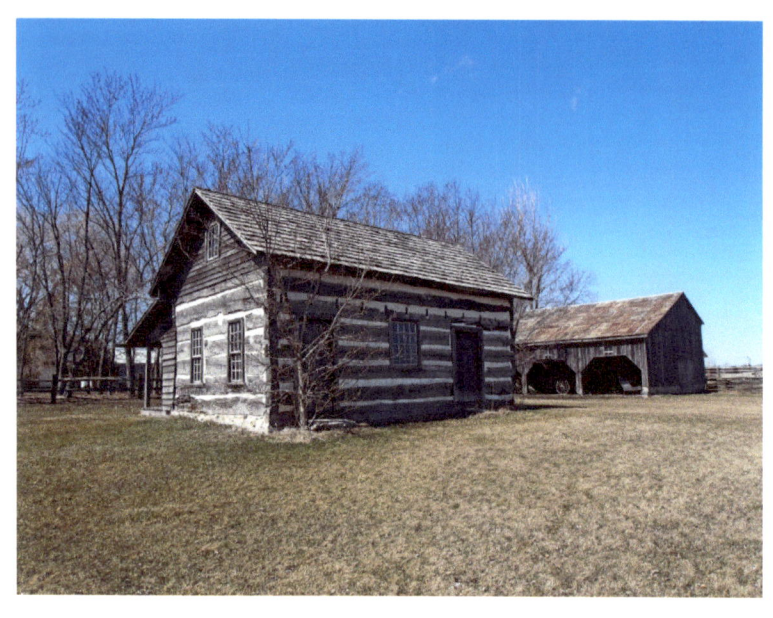

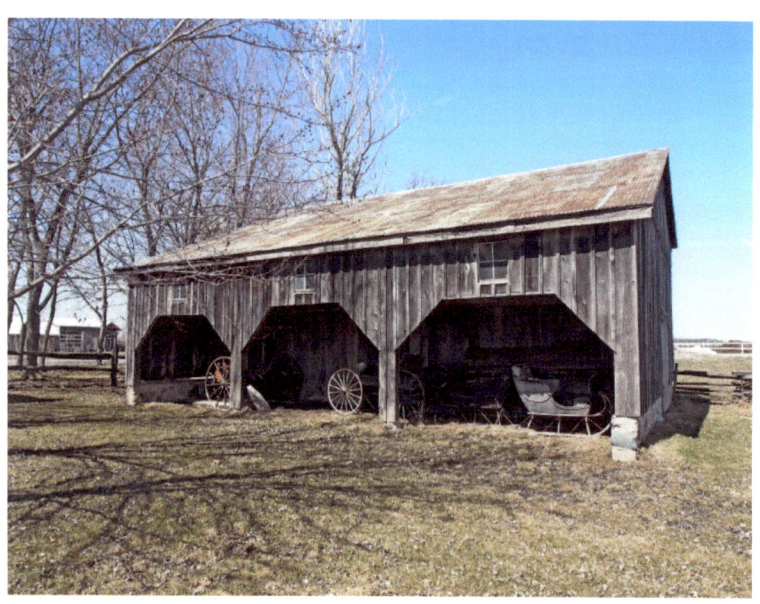

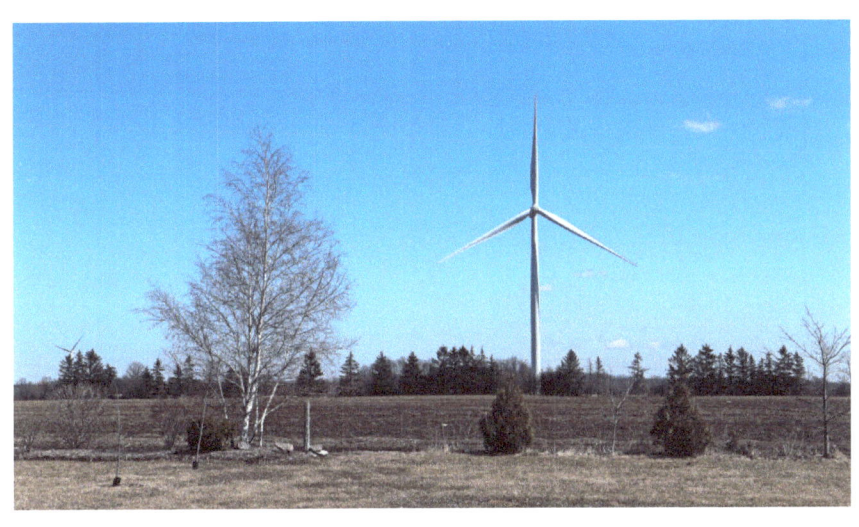

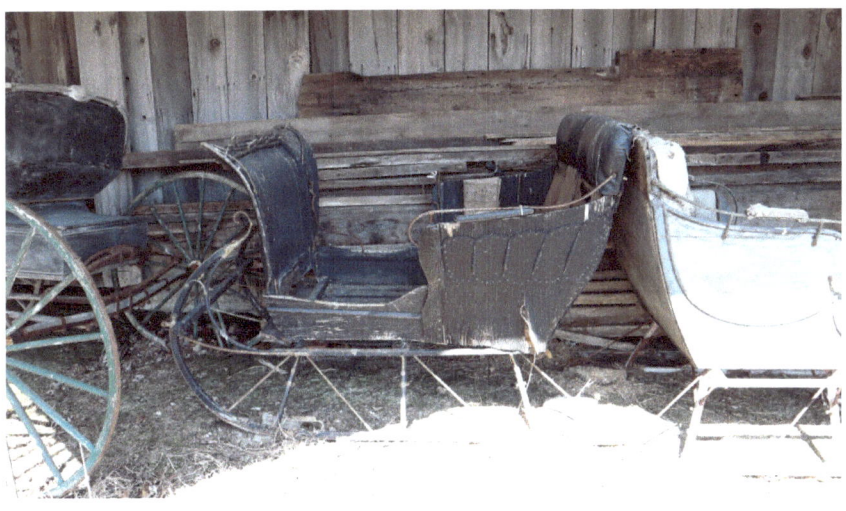

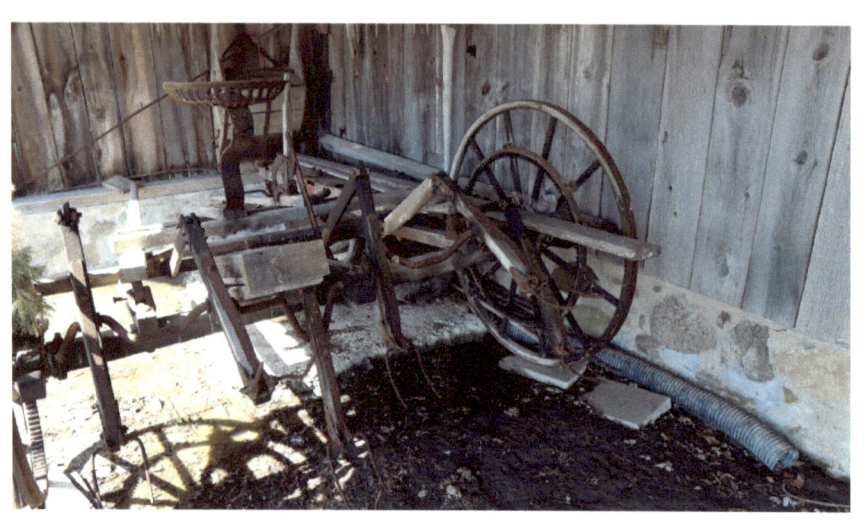

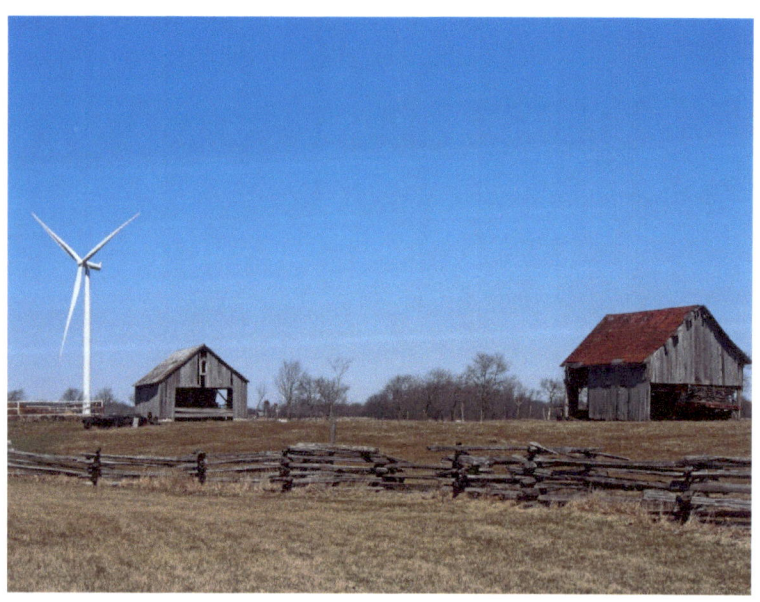

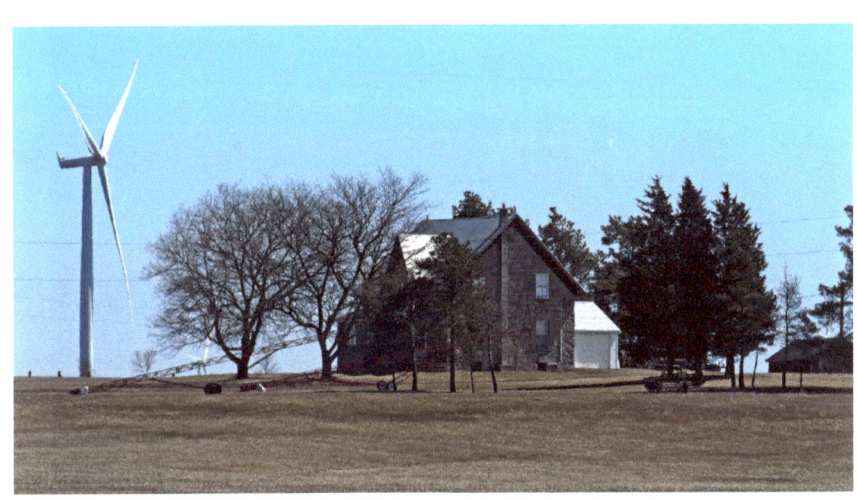
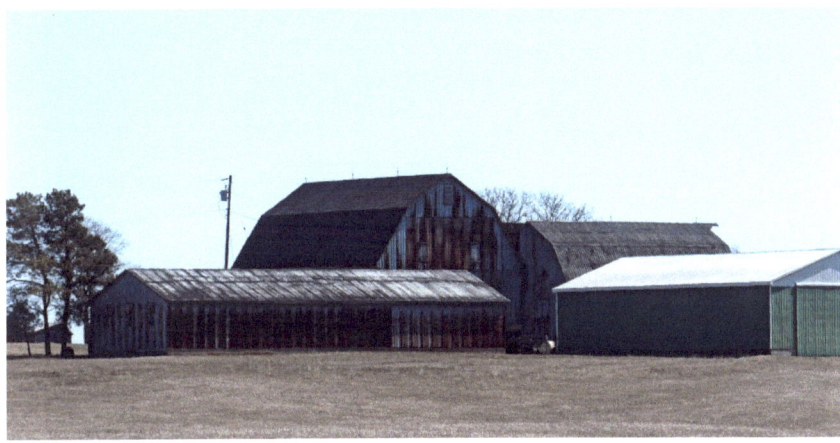
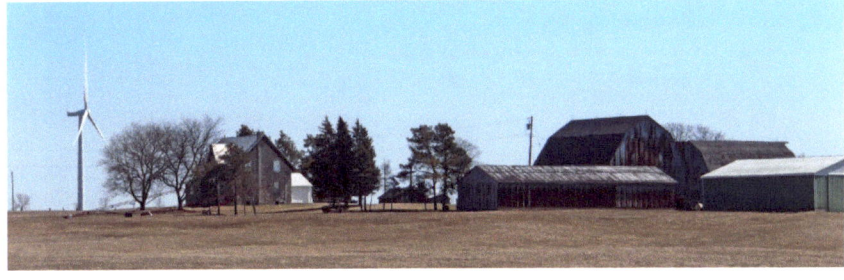

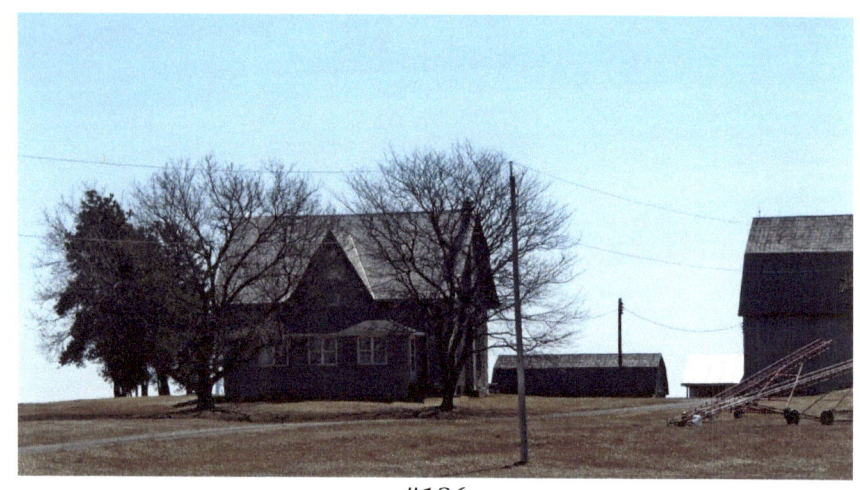

#186

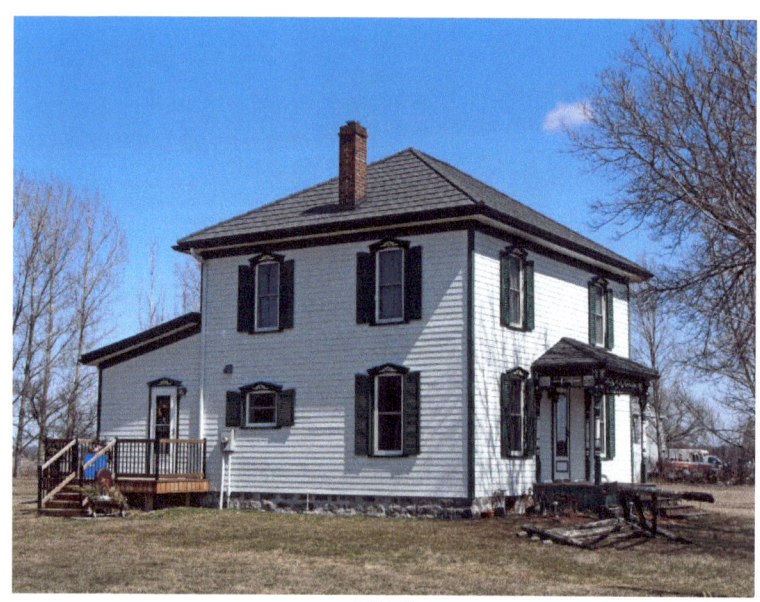

#383

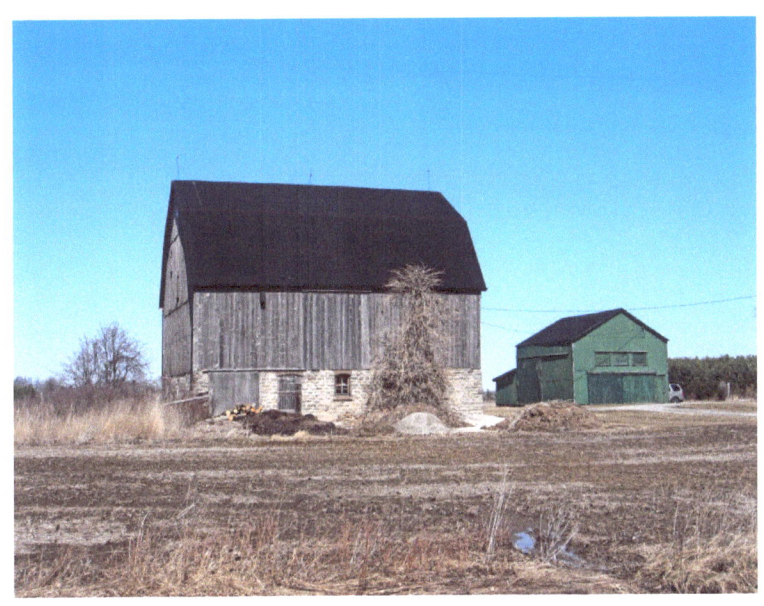

Rainham Centre

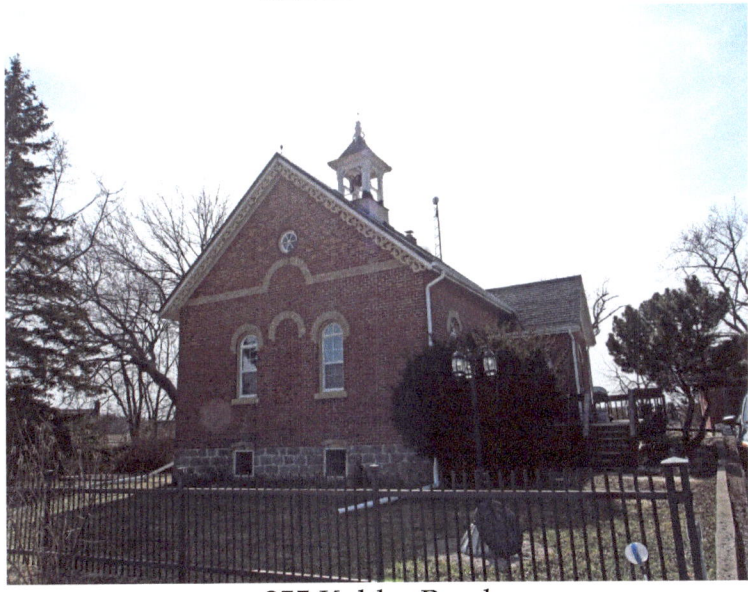

255 Kohler Road

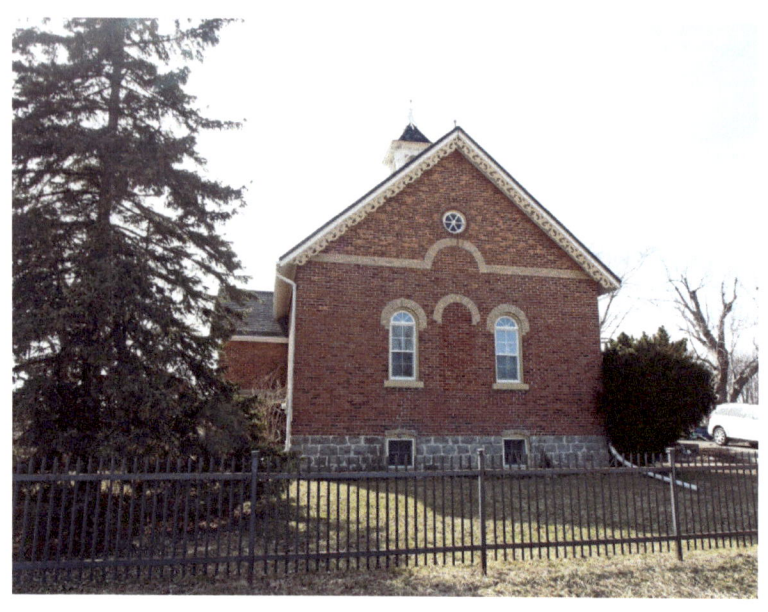

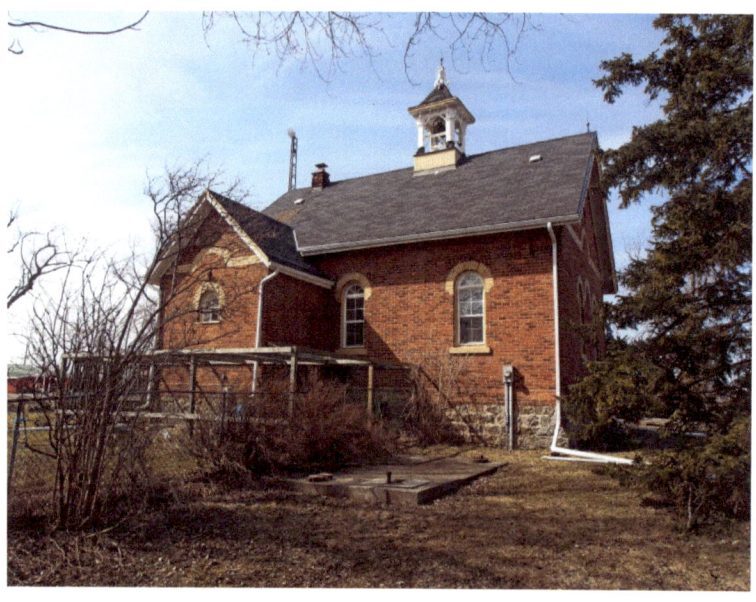

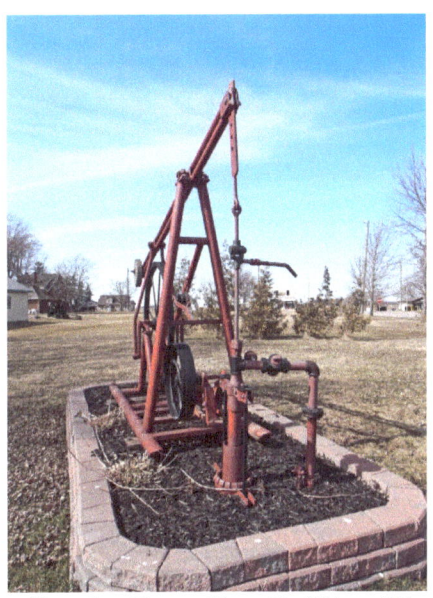

259 Kohler Road - Canadian Drilling Rig Museum

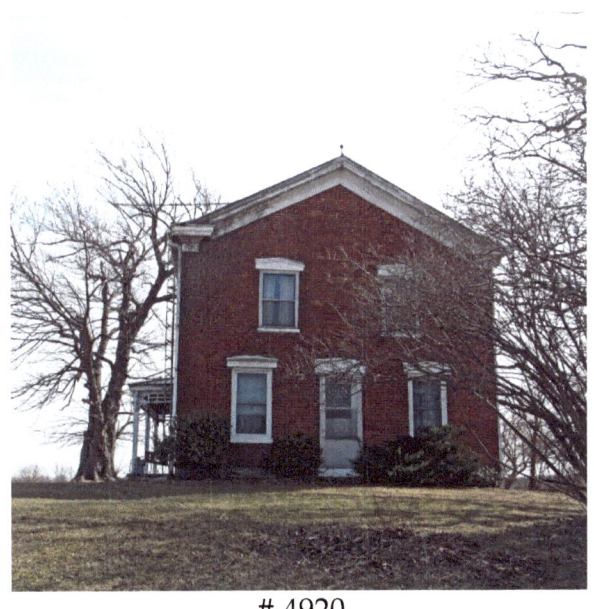

4920

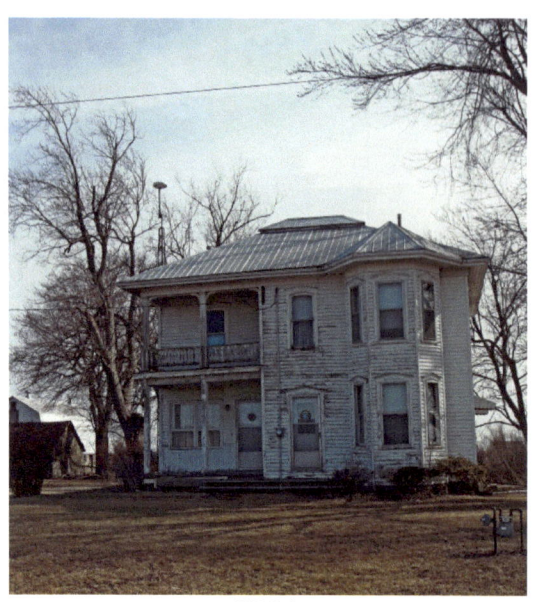

5034

Nanticoke

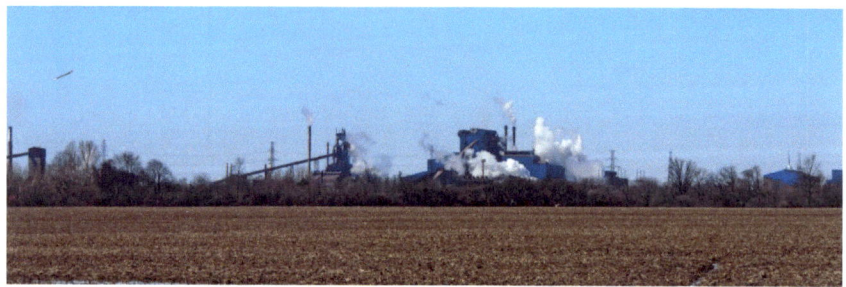

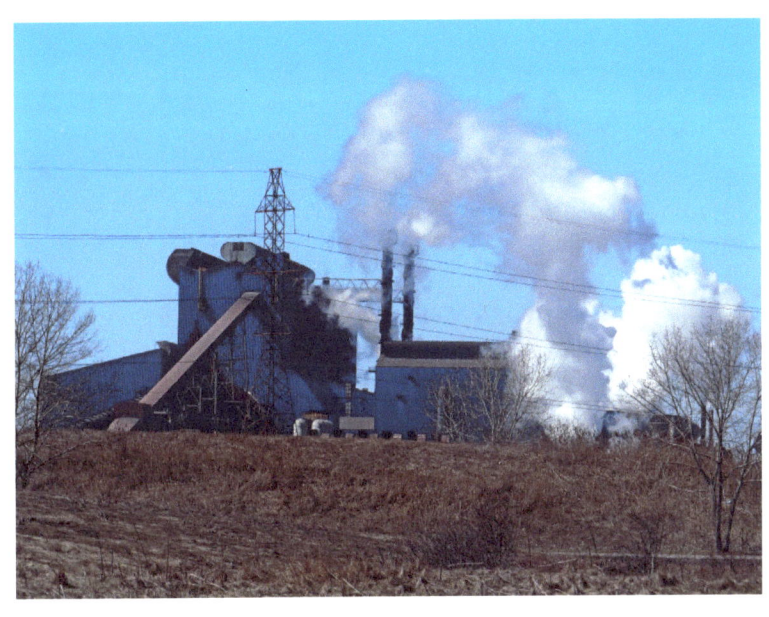

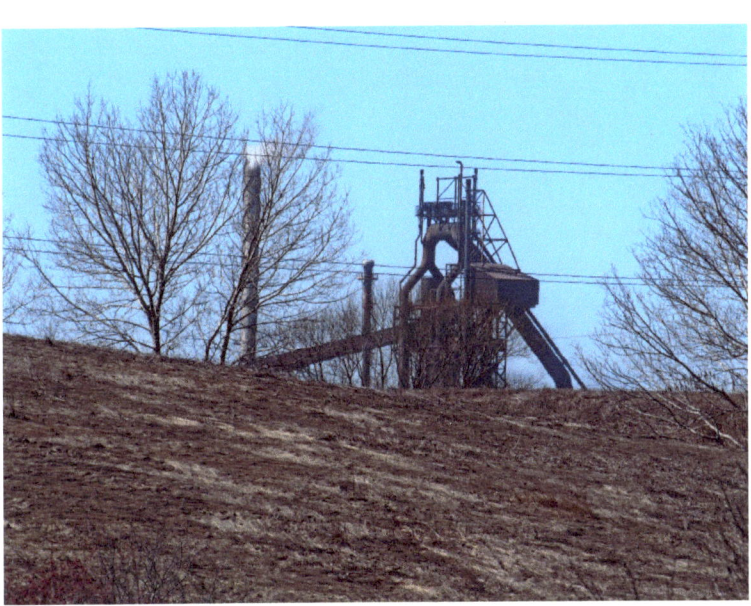

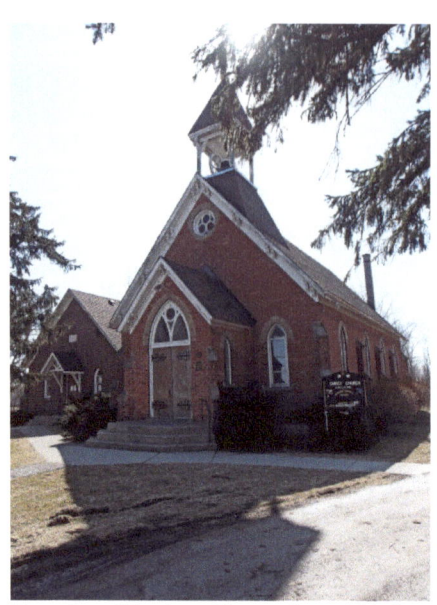

136 Rainham Road – Christ Church – 1886 – Gothic style – lancet windows, polychromatic brickwork, buttresses, belfry with bell. The parish hall was added in 1931.

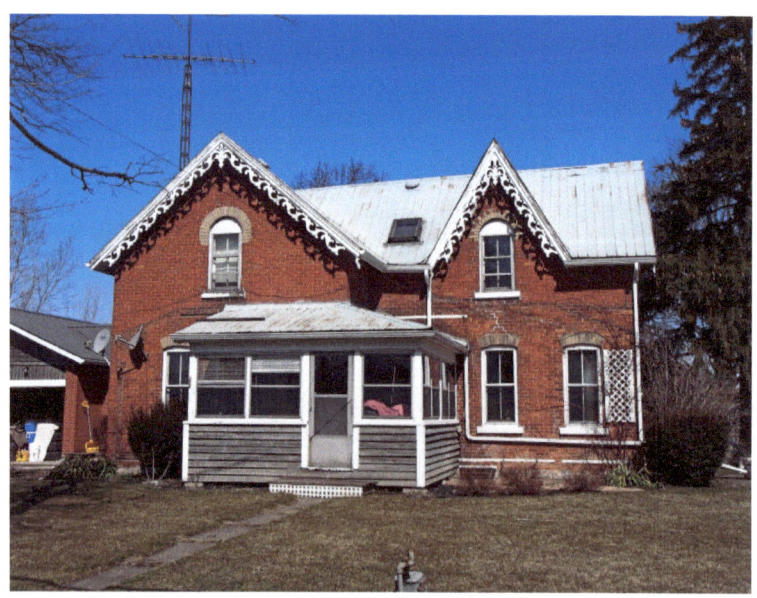

Gothic Revival – verge board trim on gables

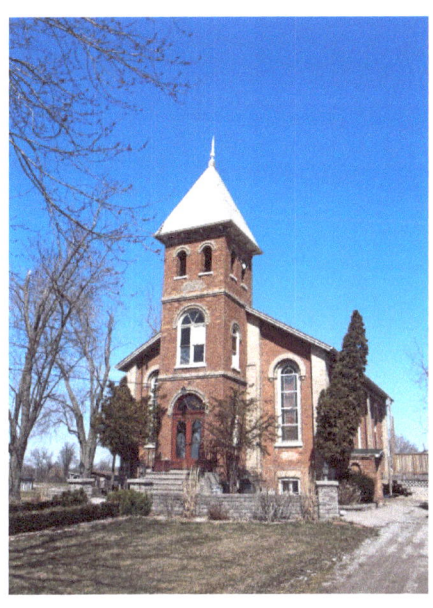

Rainham Road - Methodist Church – 1874

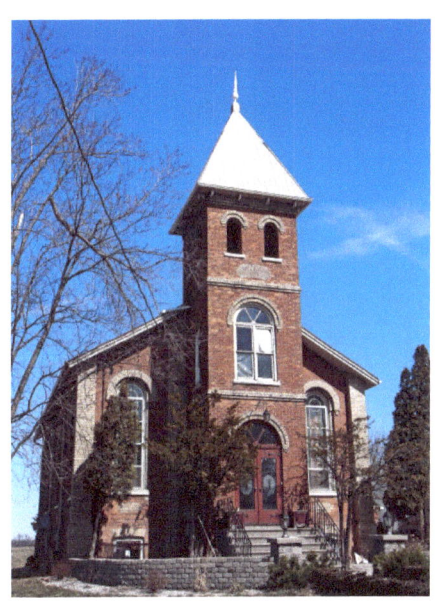

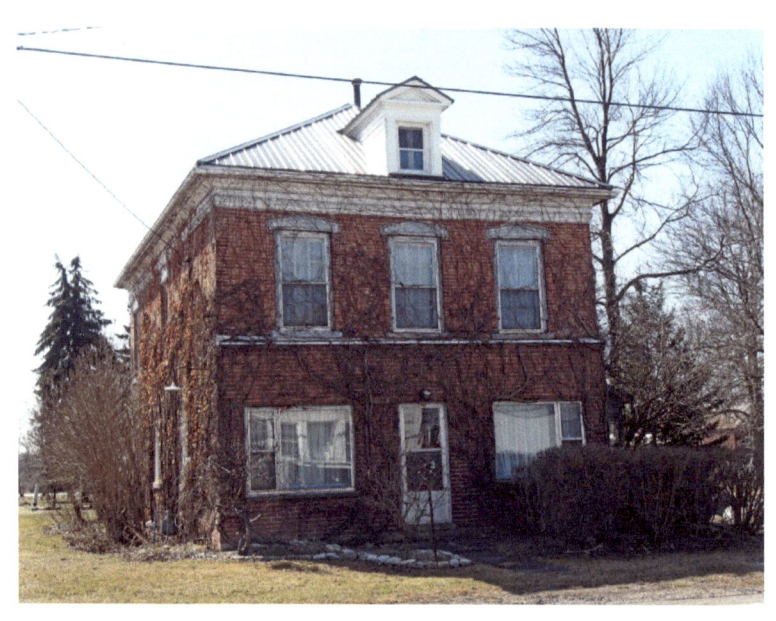

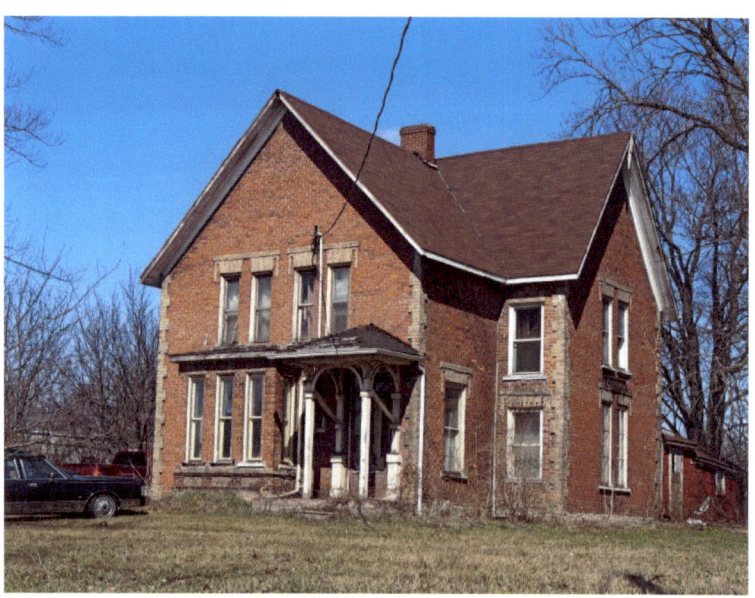

Rainham Road

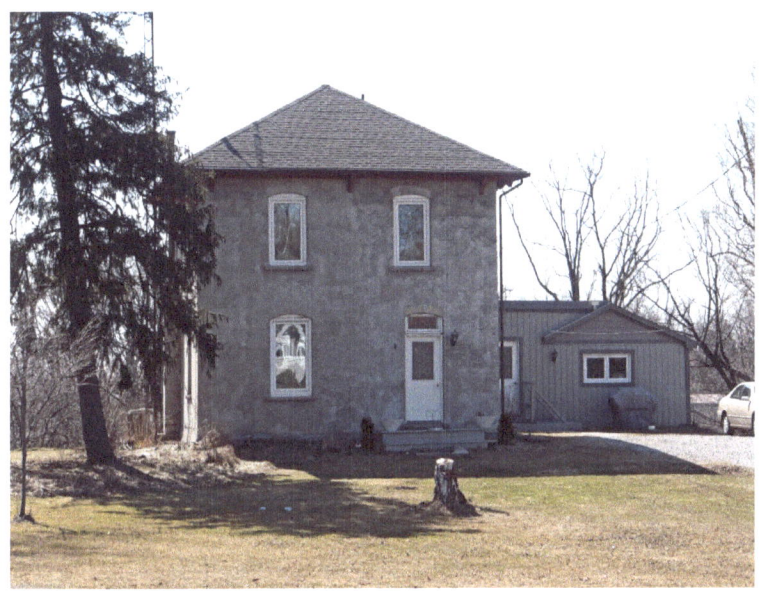

Rainham Road

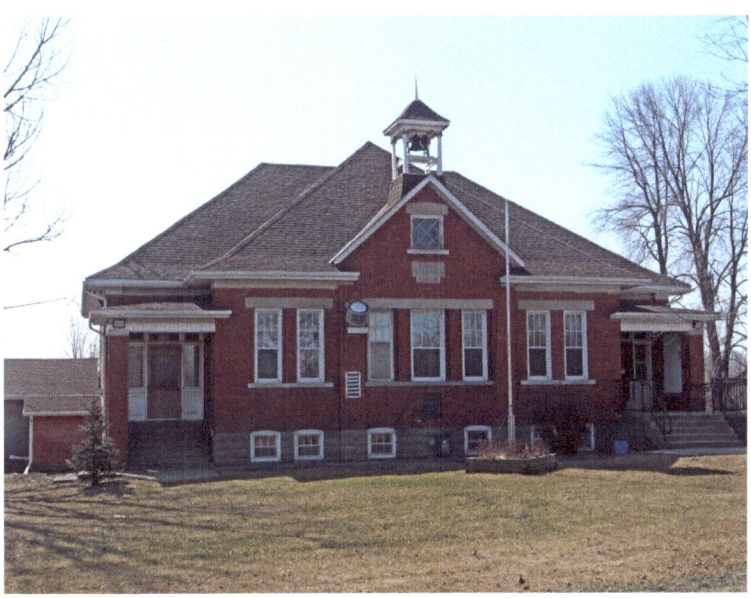

38 Rainham Road – Nanticoke Community Centre – S.S. No. 1 Walpole School – A.D. 1910

Cheapside

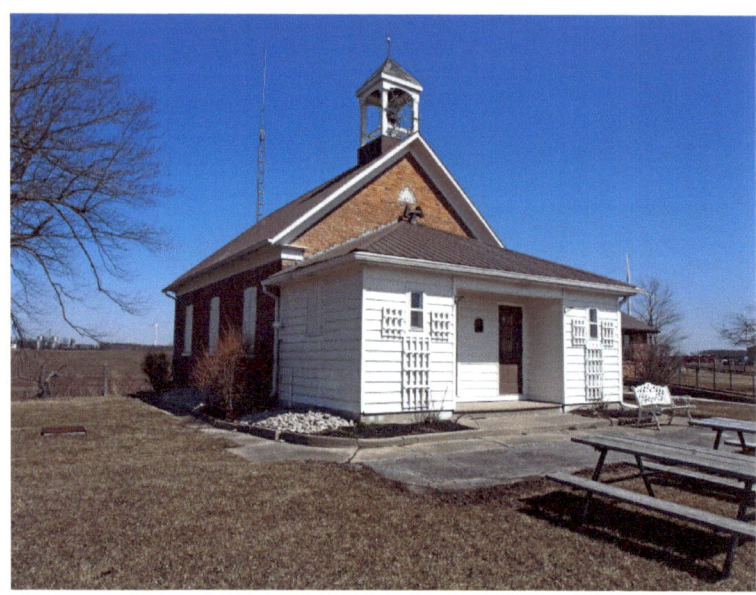

Wilson MacDonald Memorial School Museum – The original square framed school was opened on land owned by James Buckley and was replaced by this red brick one in 1872. It closed in 1965 and reopened in 1967 as a museum and memorial to Wilson MacDonald, a former student and renowned poet.

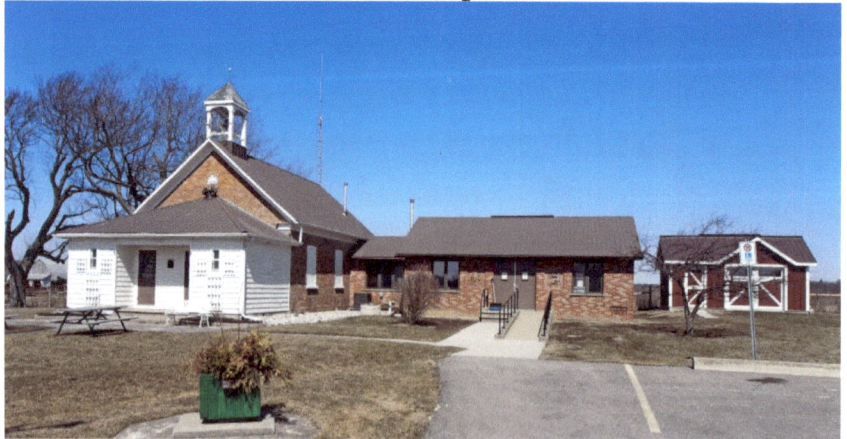

William Pugsley MacDonald (1880-1967) was born at Cheapside, established his reputation as a poet with the publication in 1926 of "Out of the Wilderness," a collection of poems. Two anthologies followed, "The Song of the Prairie Land" (1918), and "The Miracle Songs of Jesus" (1921). Among his many later works are "A Flagon of Beauty," and "Caw Caw Ballads." Although he wrote both satirical and religious poetry, he was primarily a lyric poet whose concern was for unspoiled nature.

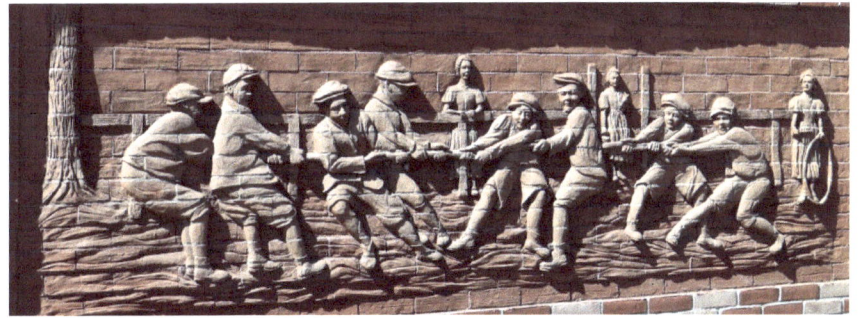

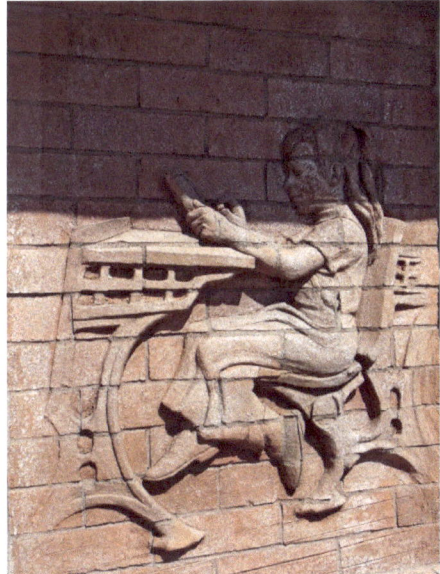 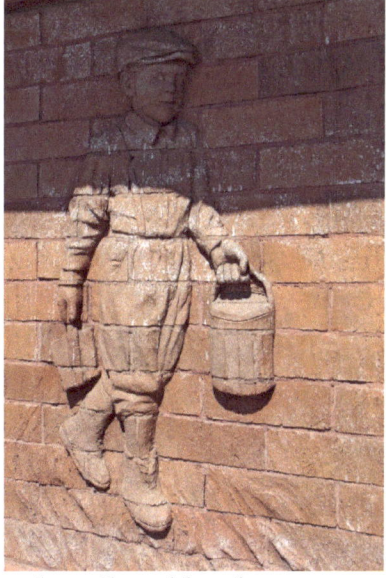

Girl at desk, boy with lunch pail and books

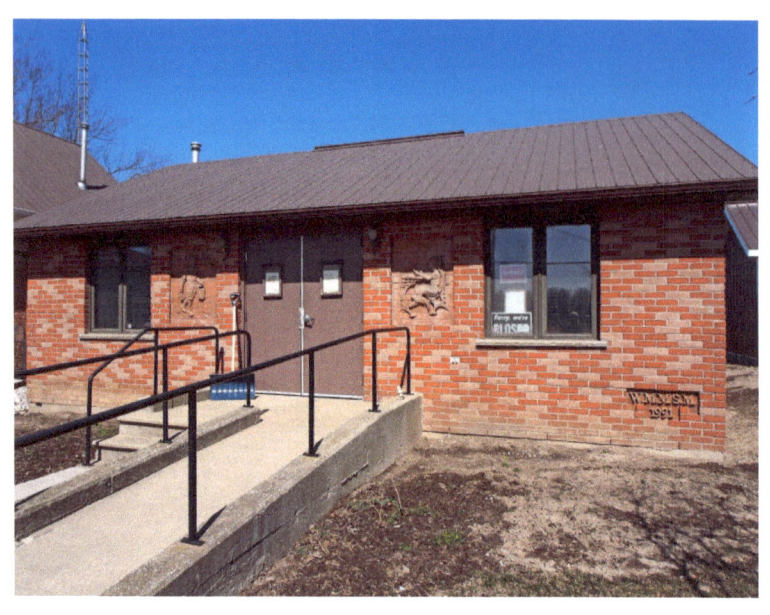

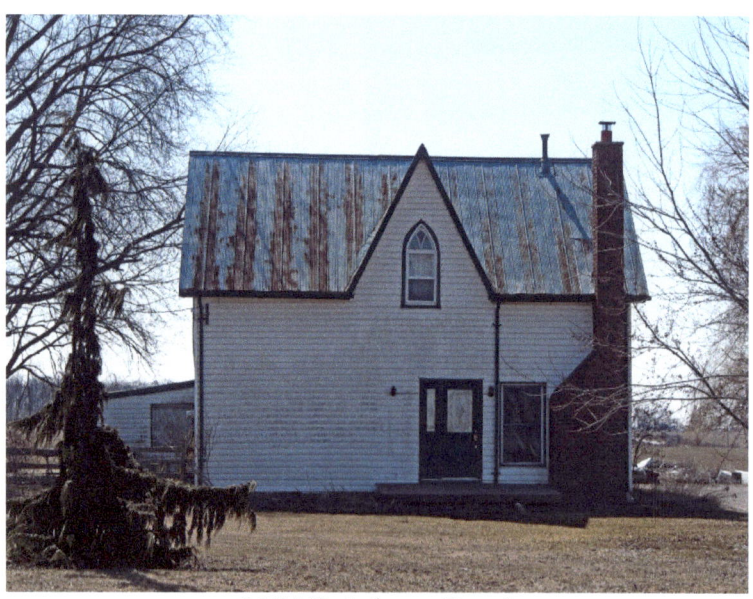

3056 Rainham Road

Selkirk

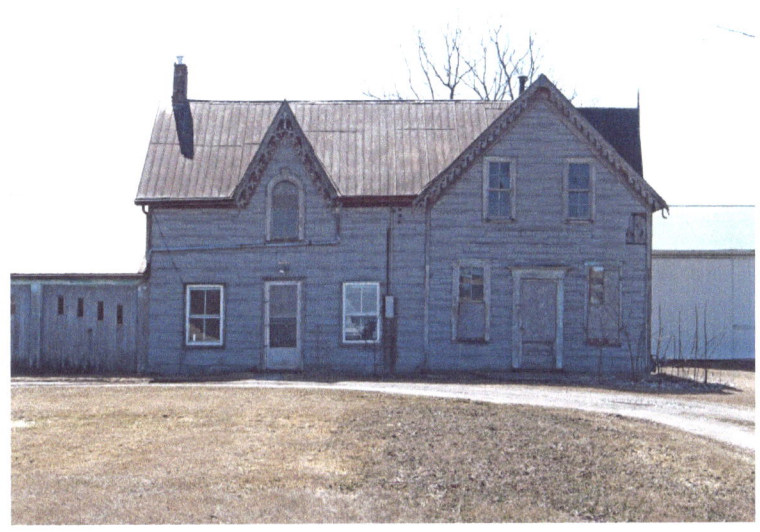

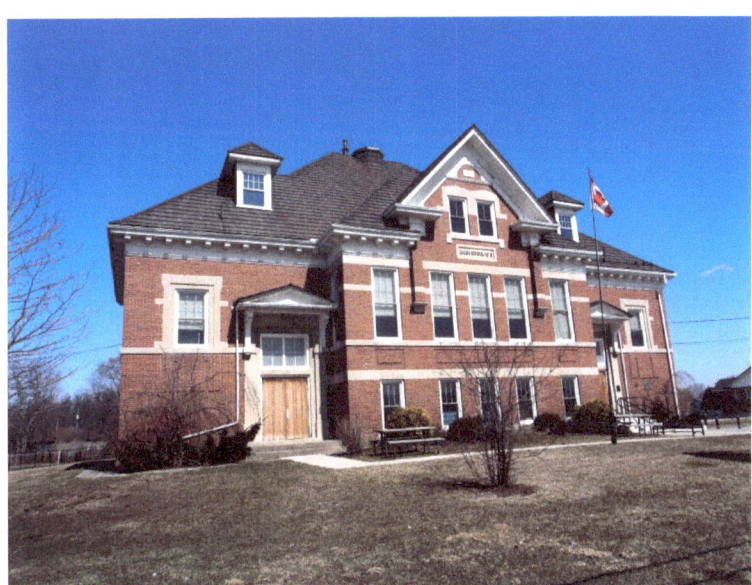

S.S. No. 3 Union School – 1918 – the school closed in 1949. It reopened in 1967 as a library and Selkirk Centennial Community Centre.

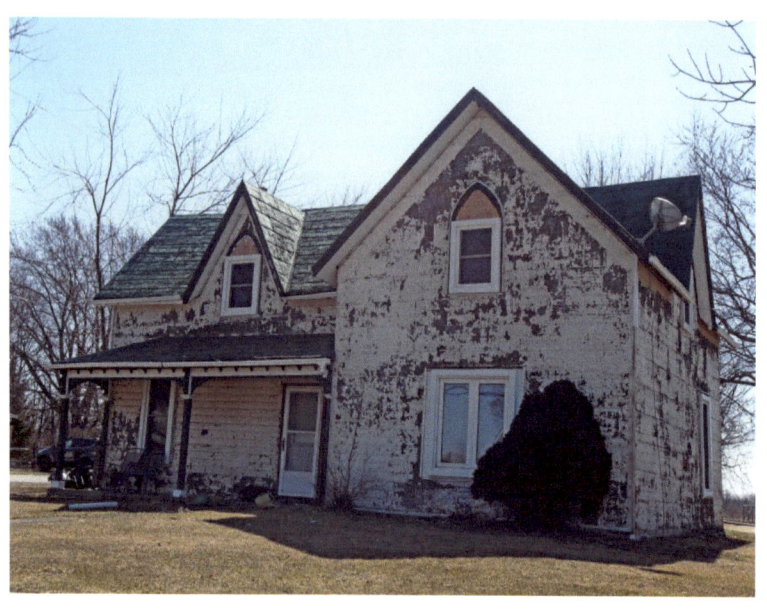

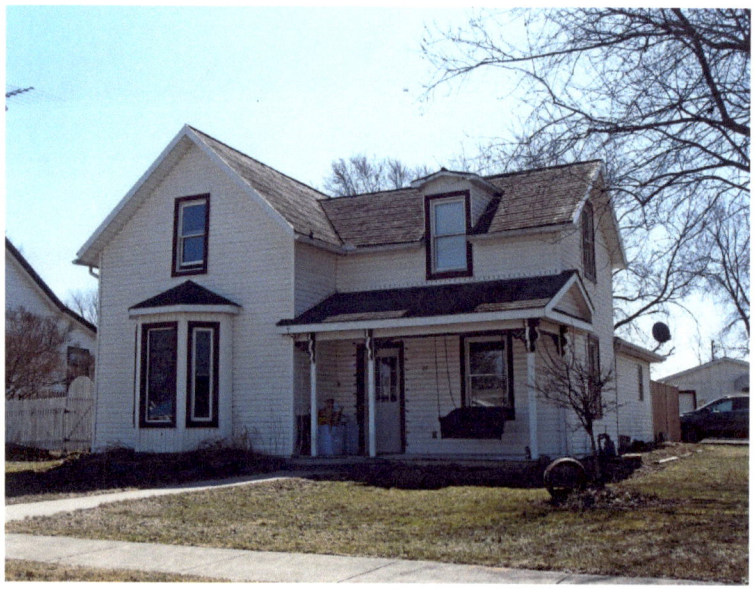

#27

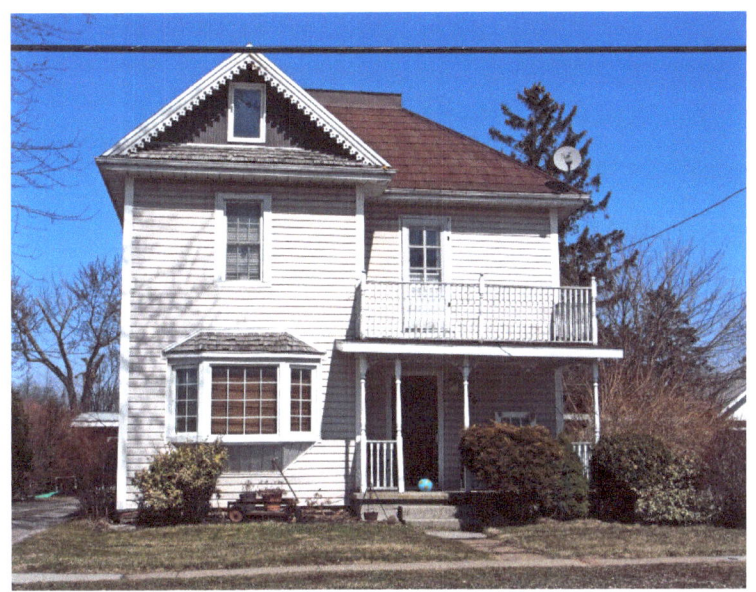

#26

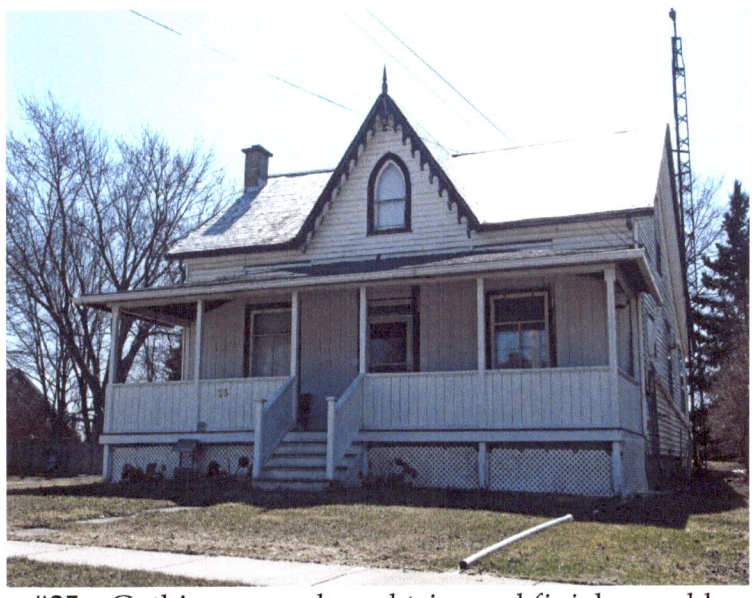

#25 – Gothic – verge board trim and finial on gable

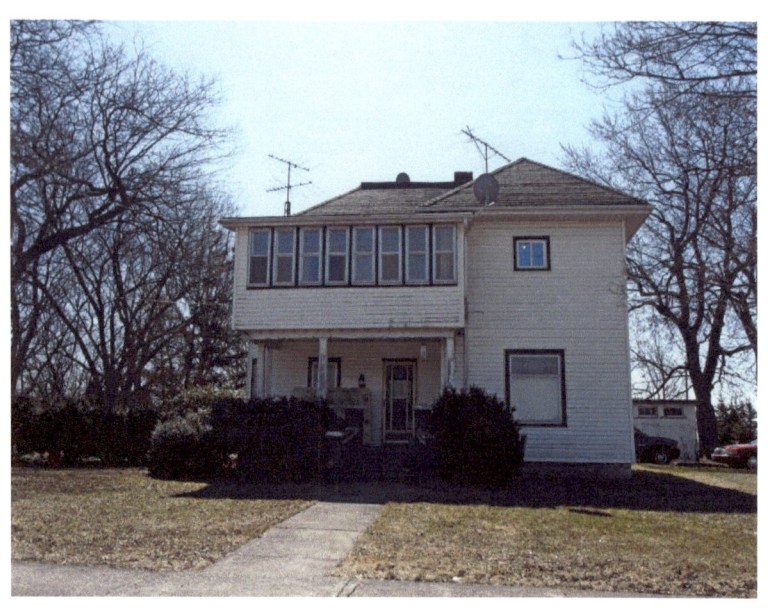

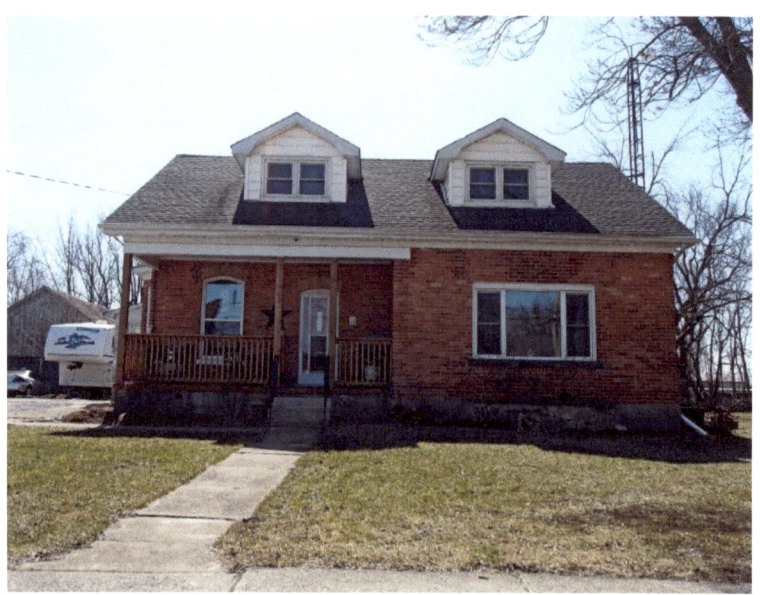

#11

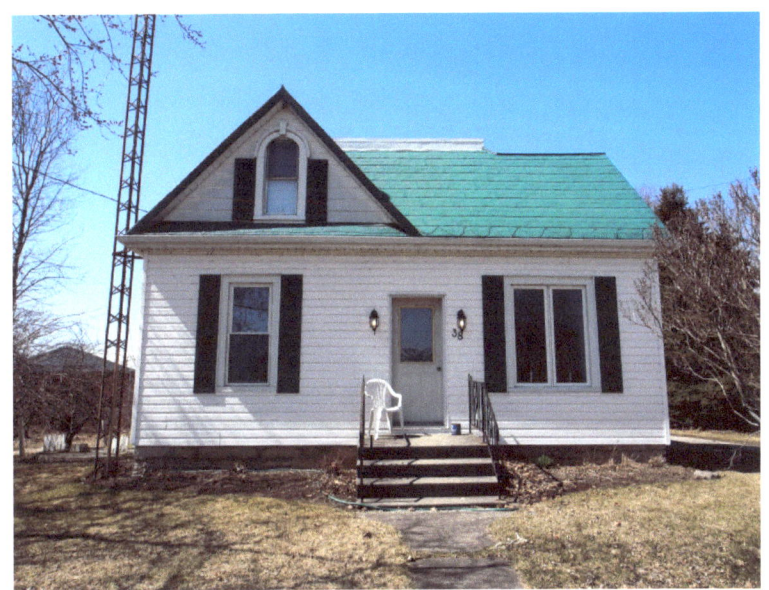

#38 Erie Street

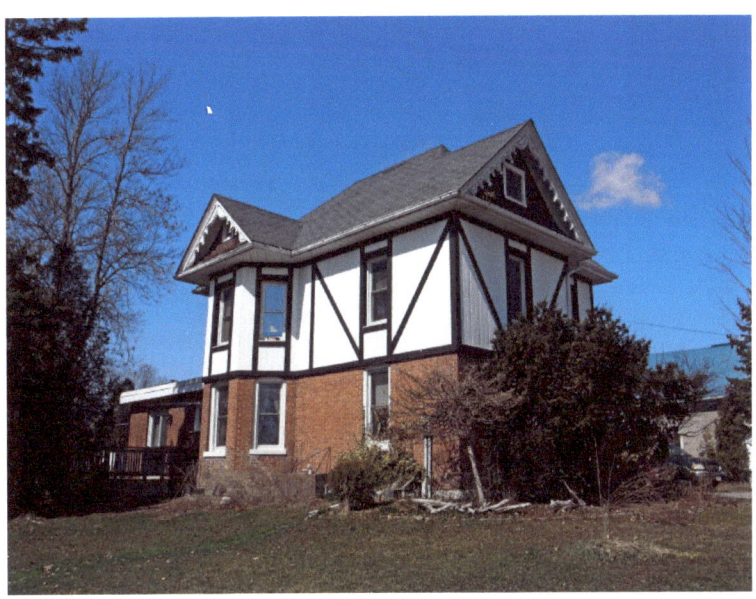

#36 Erie Street

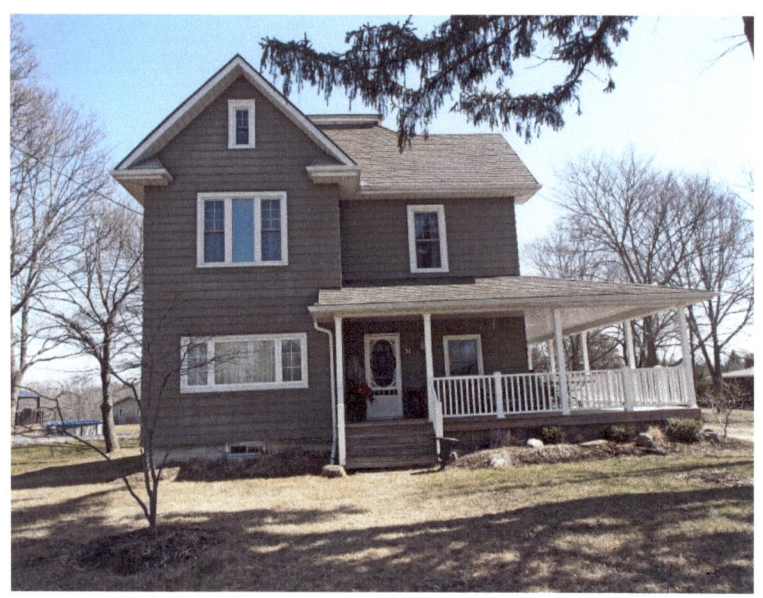

#31 Erie Street – cornice return on gable

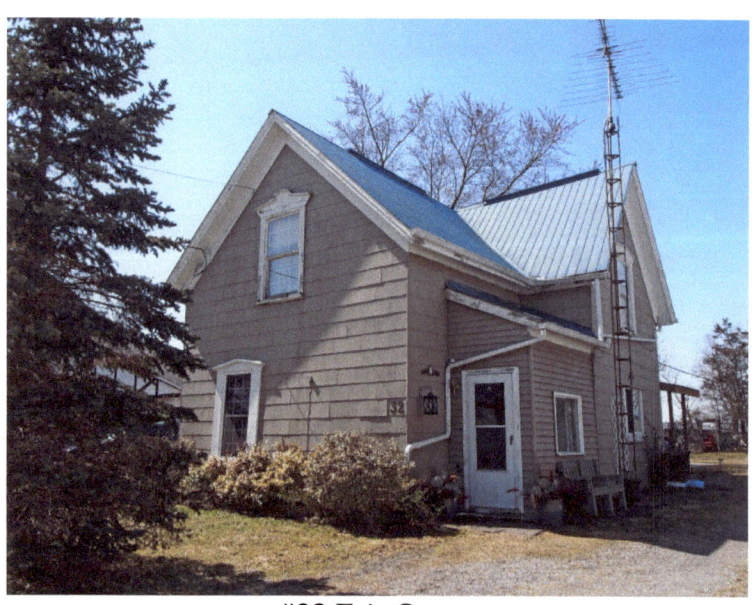

#32 Erie Street

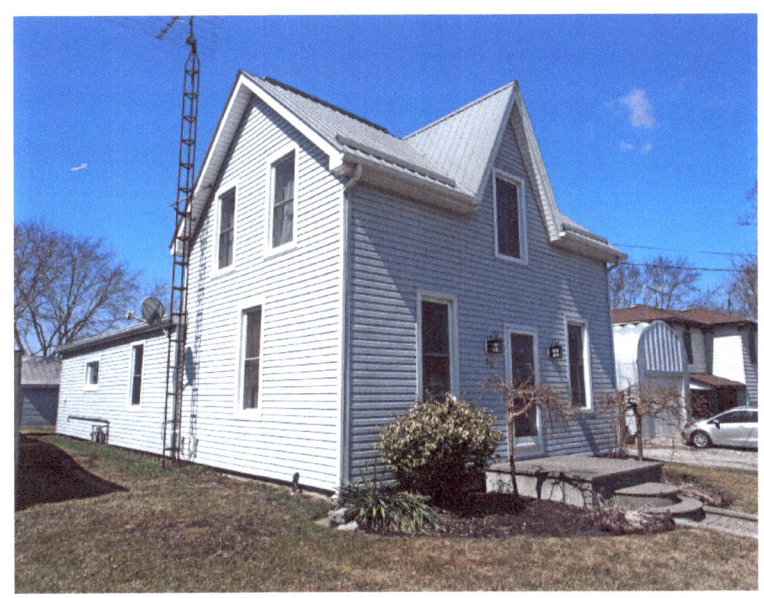

#30 Erie Street

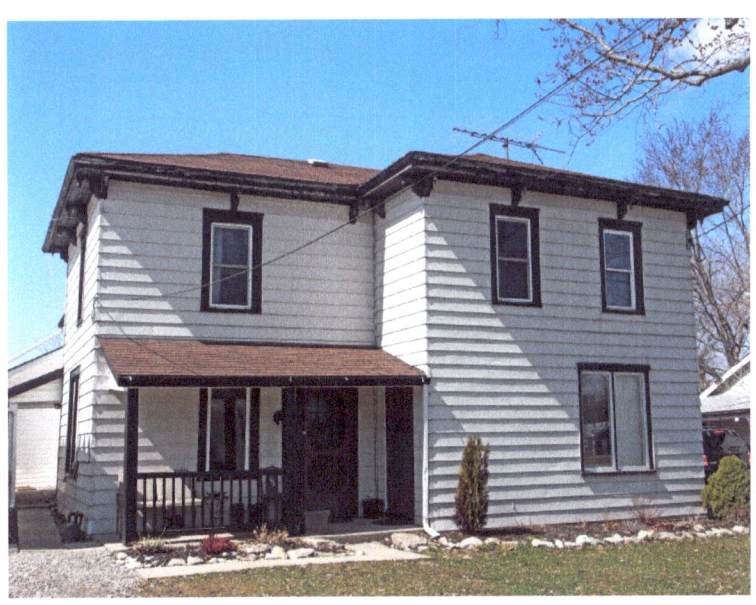

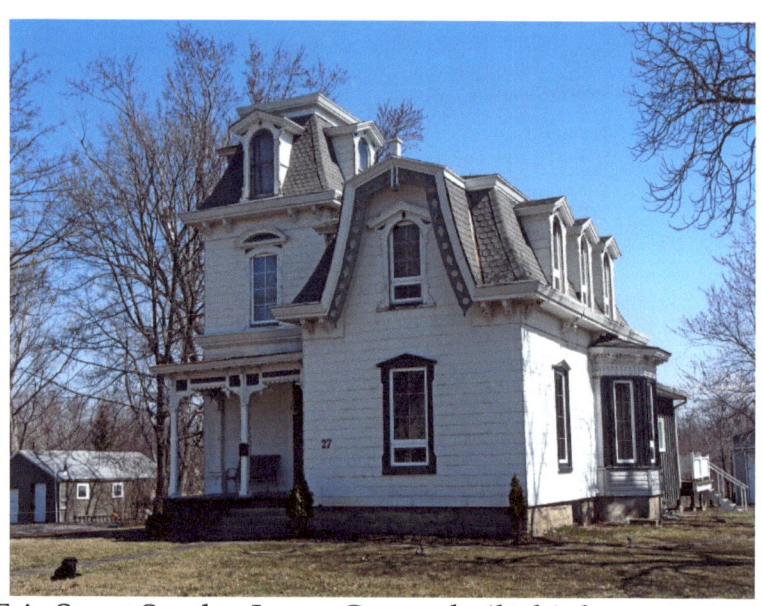

27 Erie Street South – James Cooper built this house in 1870. In 1878 he sold it to George Hoover. The frame house has irregular massing and is in the Second Empire style. It has an over-sized horseshoe dormer with bargeboard and finial, elaborate window molds with pediments. The three-storey tower has four dormers in the mansard roof. The Fess family purchased it in 1947.

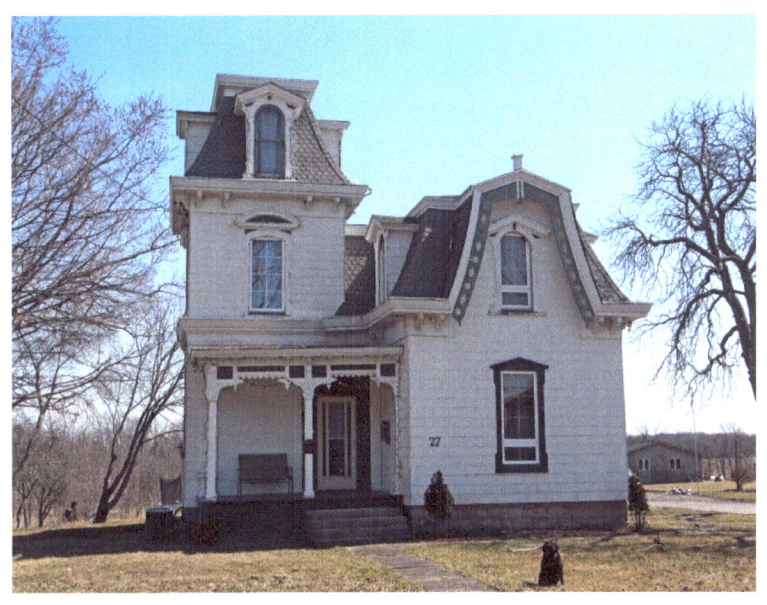

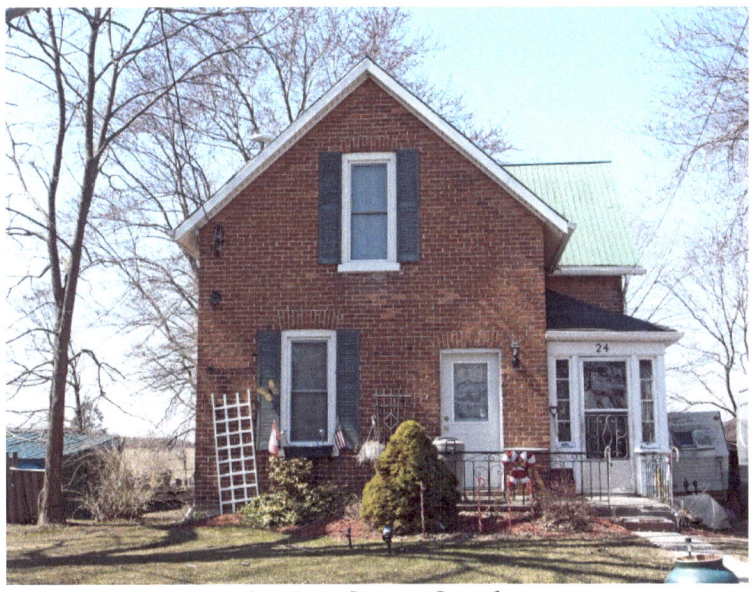

24 Erie Street South

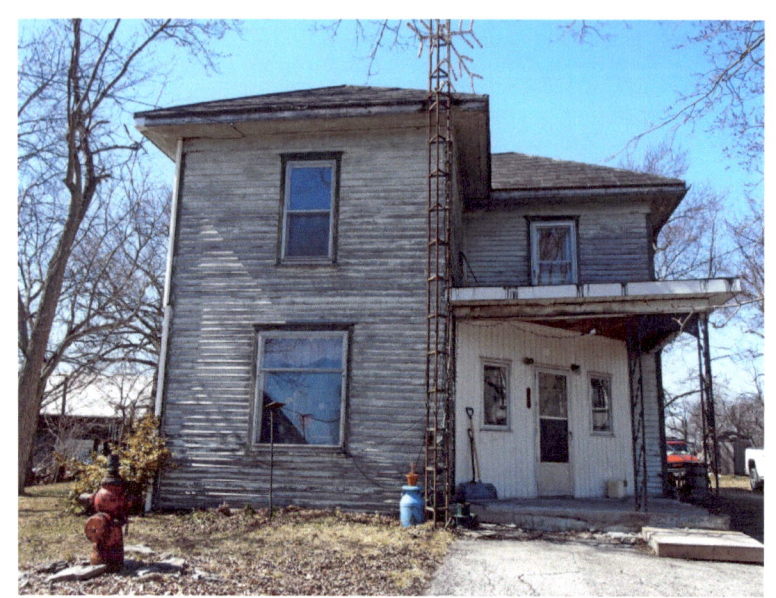
Erie Street South

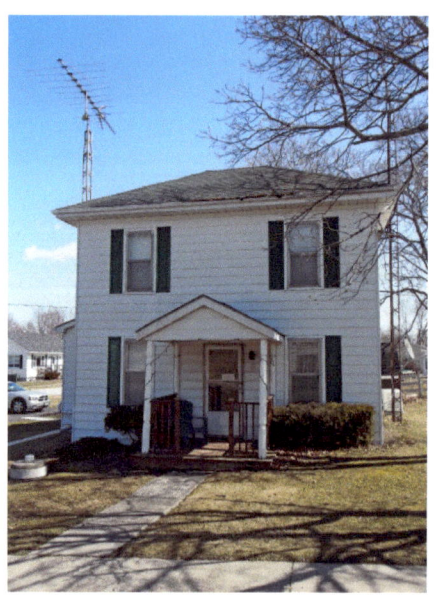
11 Erie Street South

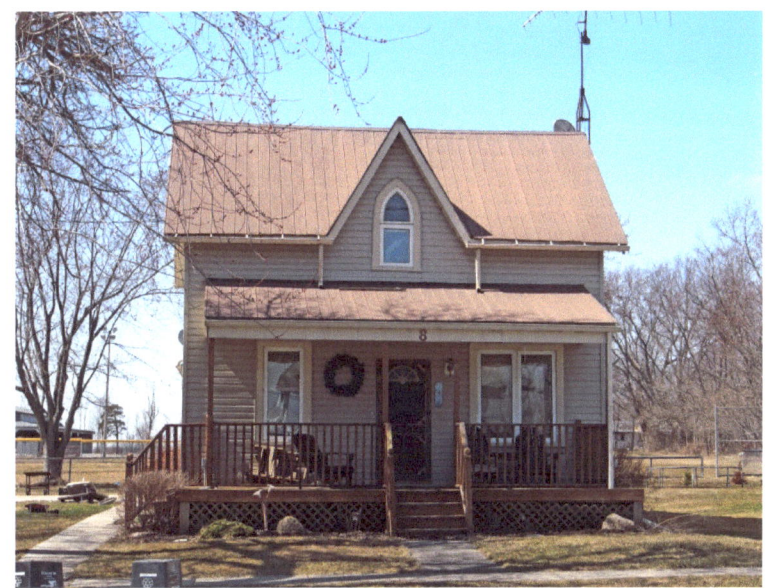

8 Erie Street South

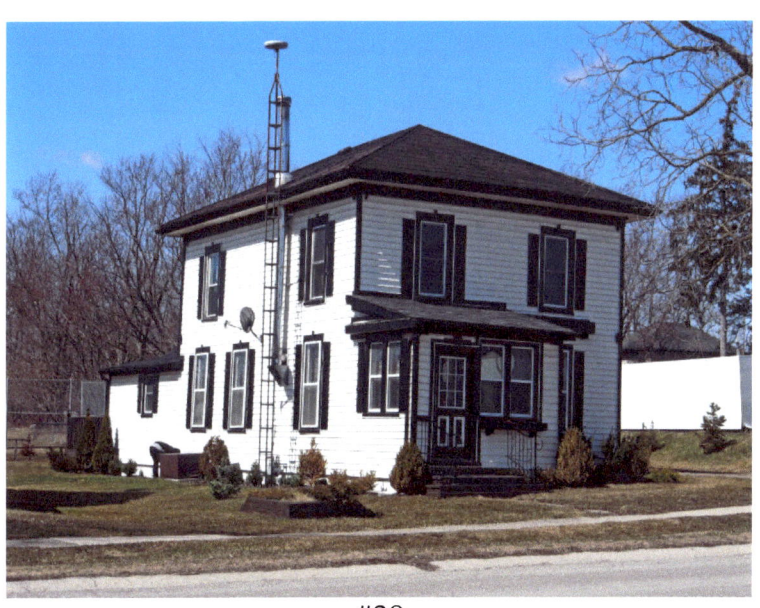

#38

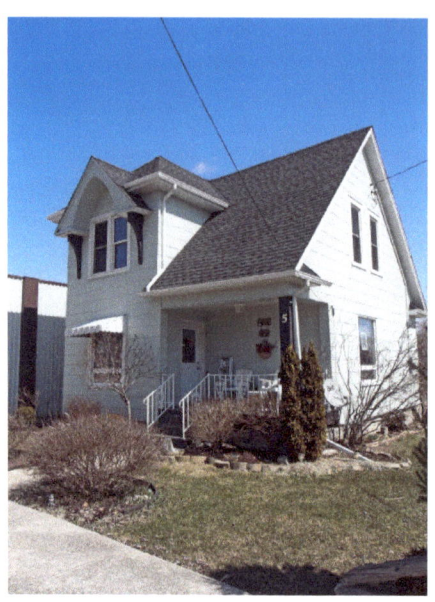

#3

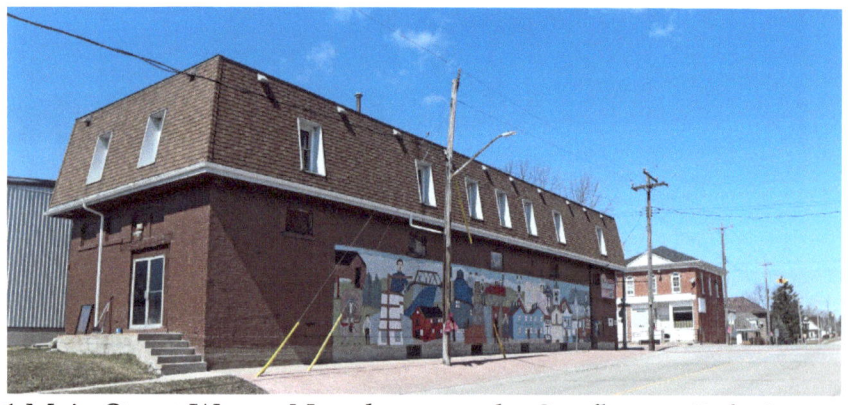

1 Main Street West – Now home to the Sunflower Café, it was the Selkirk Deli and Family Restaurant. There was a butter factory here, later a drug store, bake shop, billiard hall, post office, and barber shop.

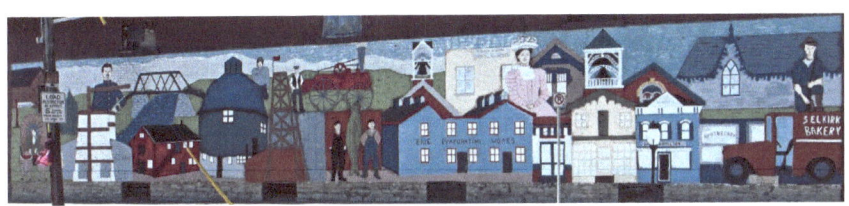

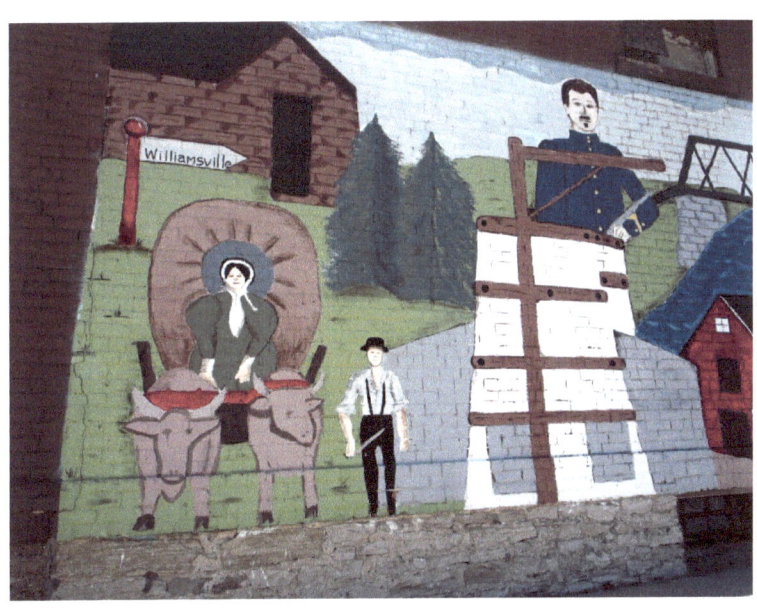

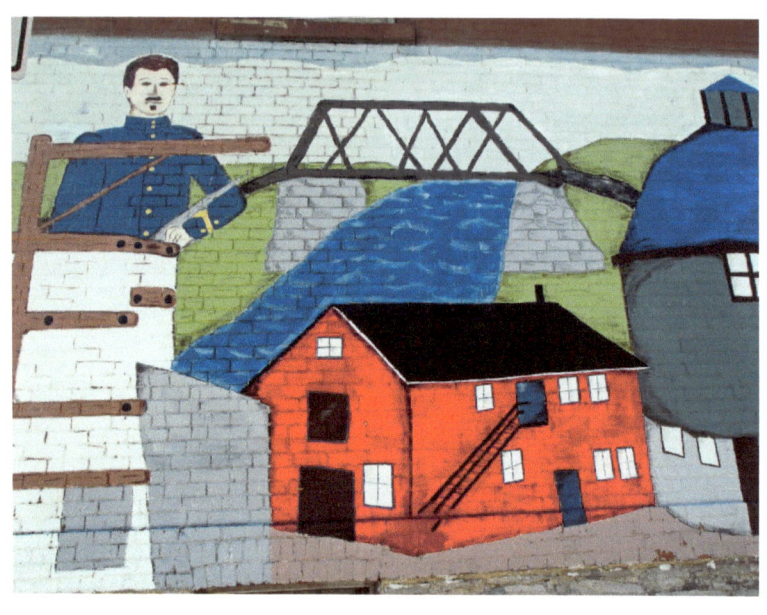

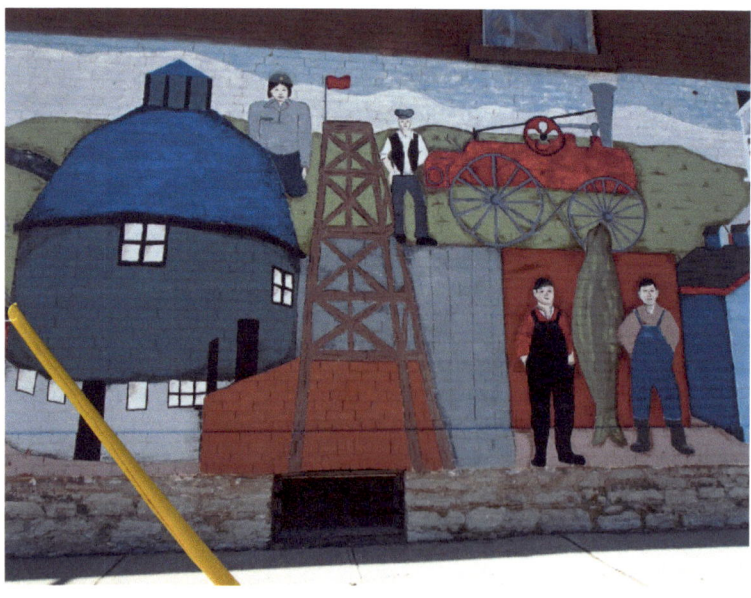

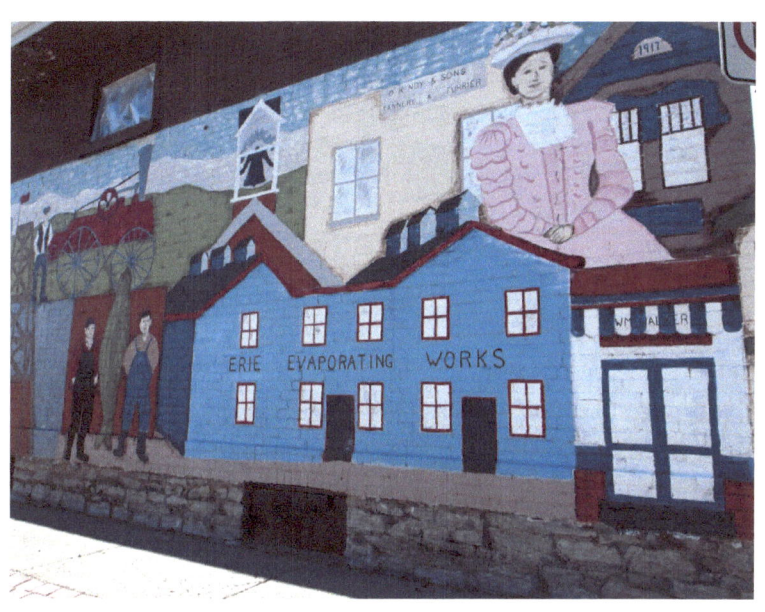

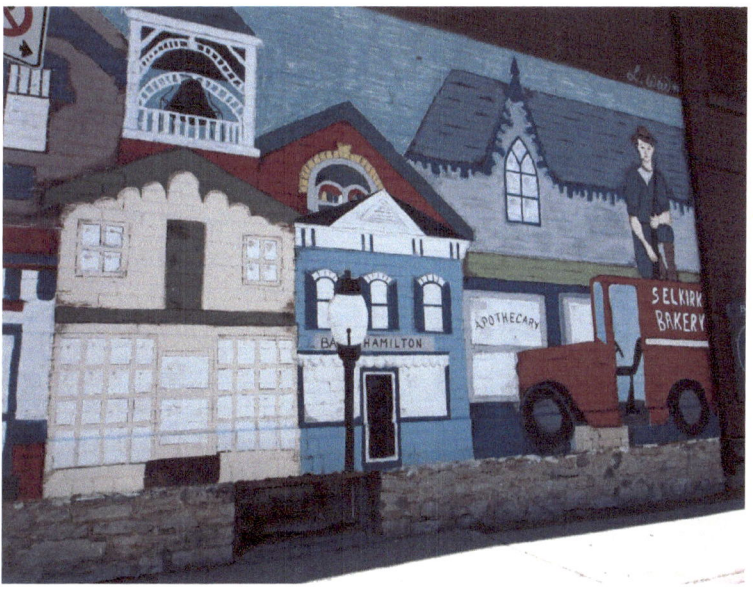

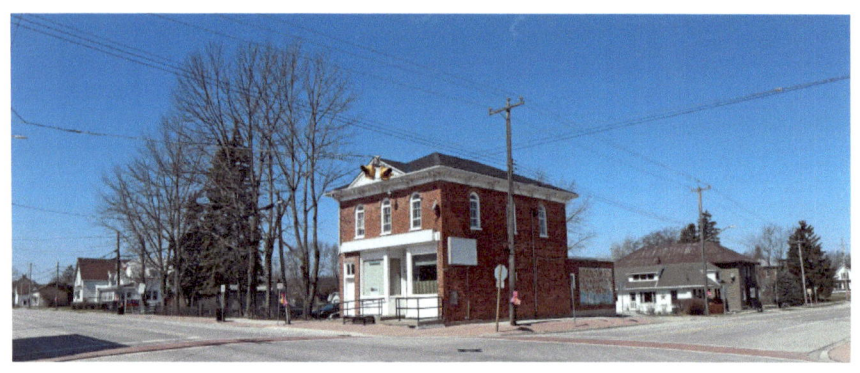

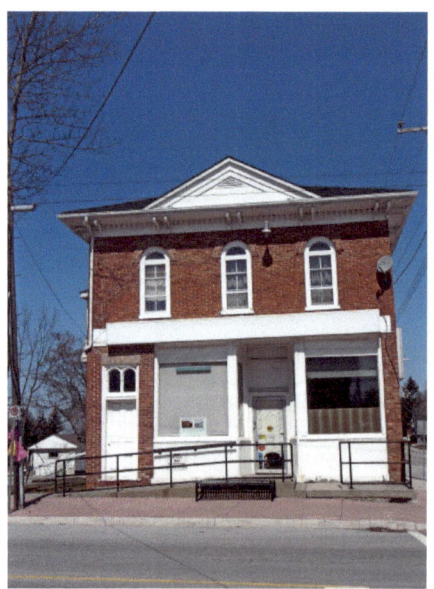

Erie Street North

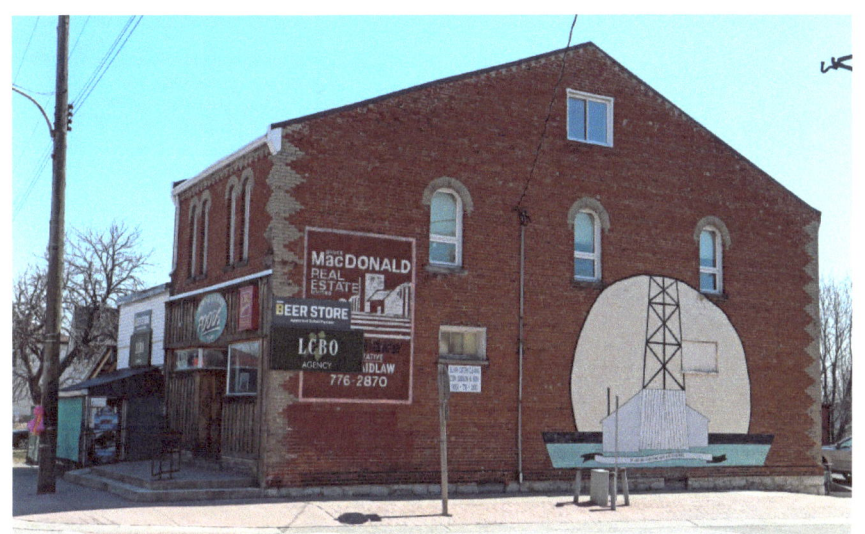

4 Main Street East – Town & Country Foods

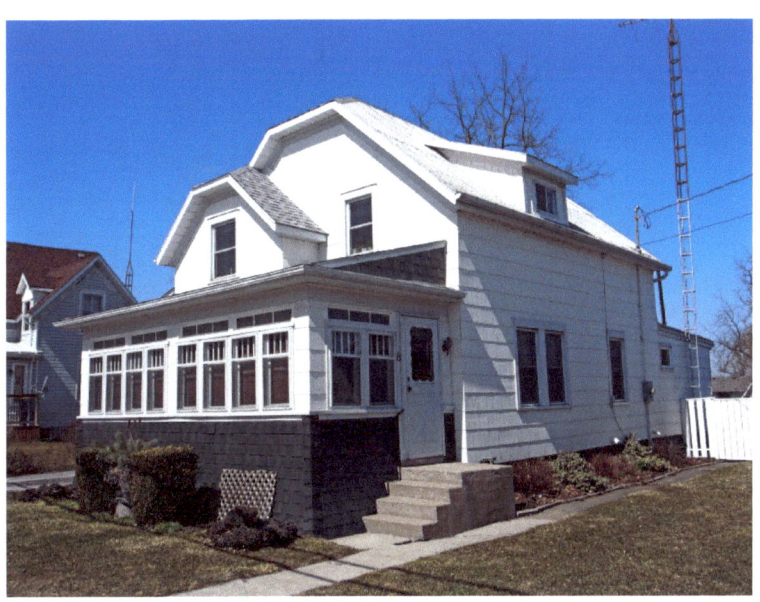

#8 Erie Street North – chipped gables, dormers

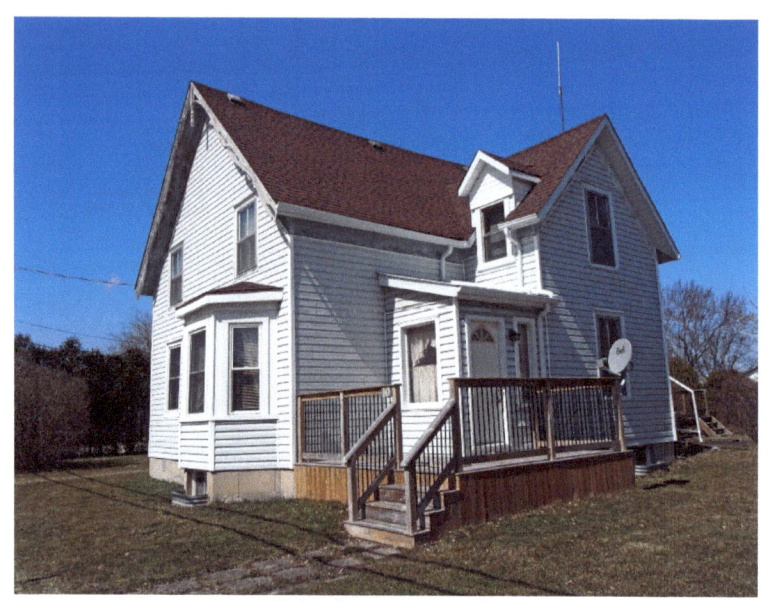

Erie Street North

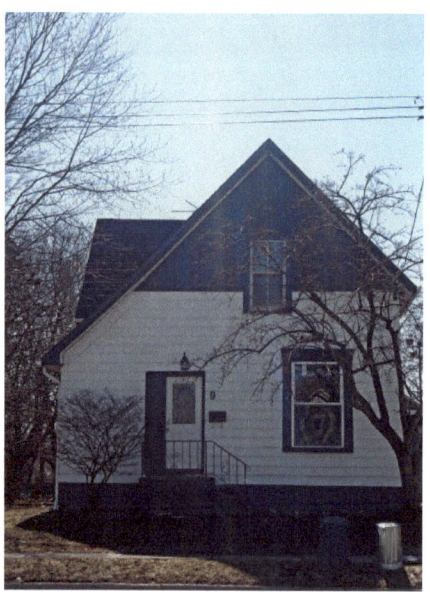

#9 Erie Street North

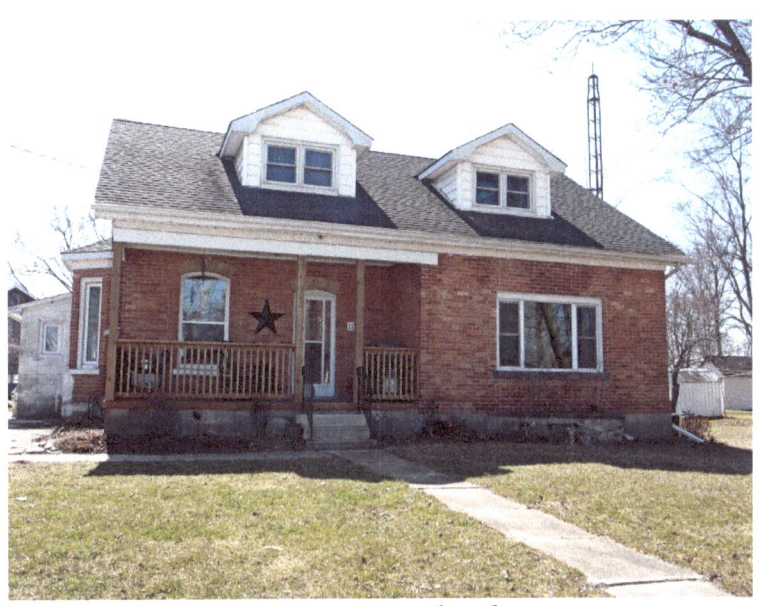

#11 Erie Street North - dormers

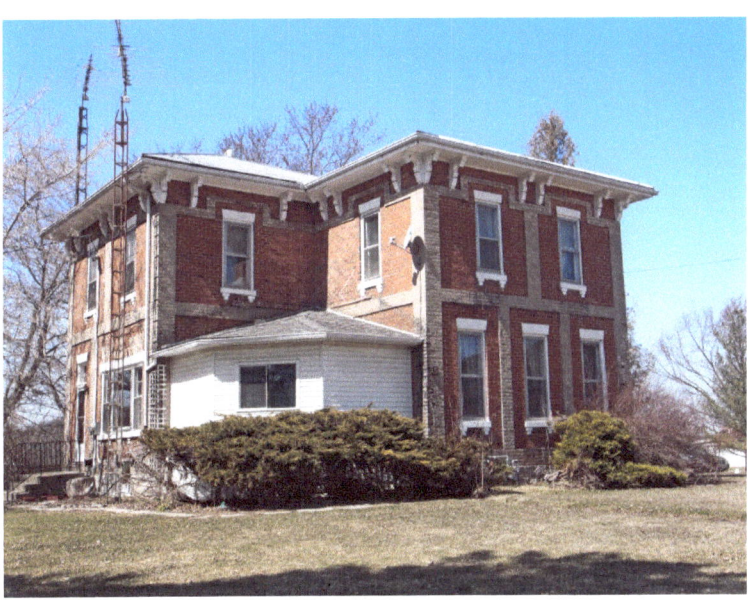

#15 Erie Street North – Italianate, hipped roof, cornice brackets, quoins, banding

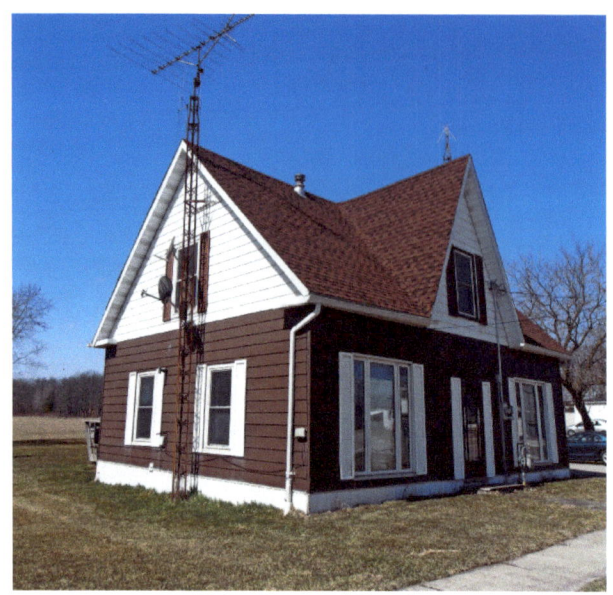
Erie Street North

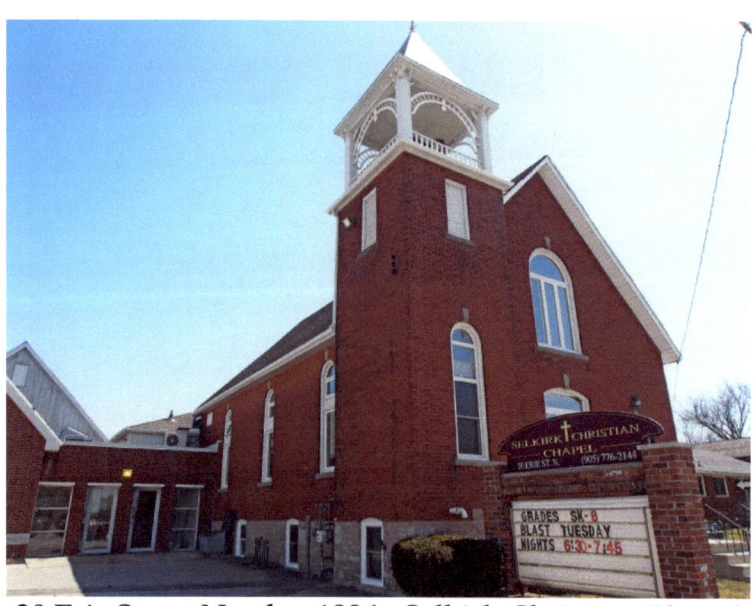
20 Erie Street North – 1896 - Selkirk Christian Chapel

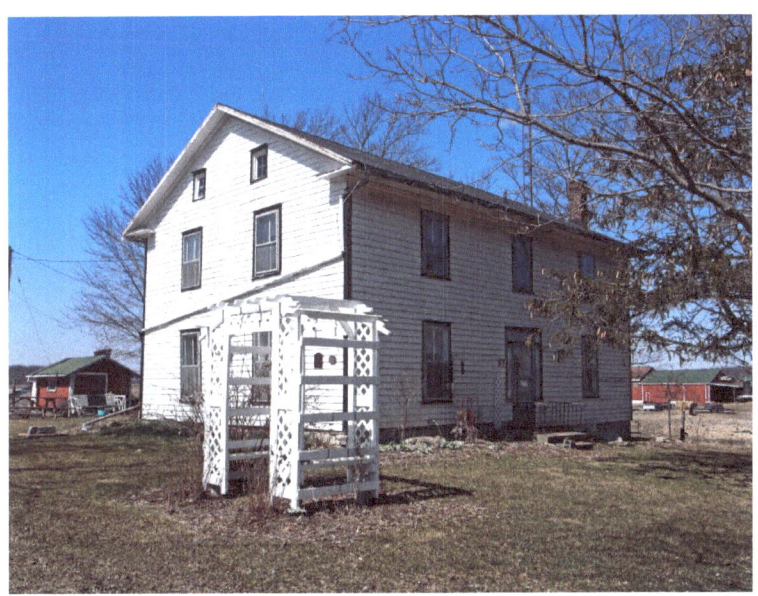

57 Erie Street North – circa 1780 – was constructed of sun-dried mud blocks made from pea straw and clay trampled by oxen. In 1817, Elizabeth (Hoover) Knisley received the land; the house remained in the family until 1903. In 1851, weatherboard was added to preserve the façade. The Lindsay family took over the house in 1905. The house has a central hall plan with a rear kitchen extension. The doors and windows were deeply set to accommodate the blocks (very noticeable in the two windows in the gable).

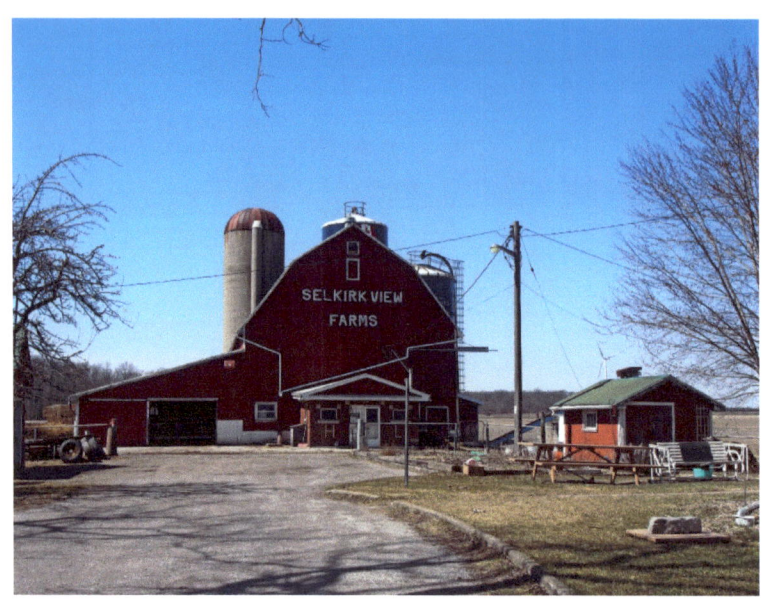

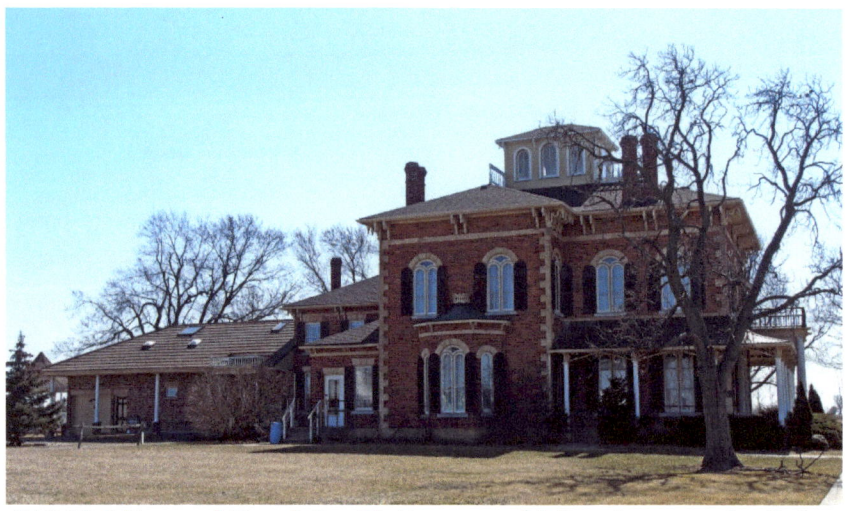

740 Haldimand Road 3 – Cottonwood Mansion was built by William Holmes circa 1860 in the Italianate architectural style.

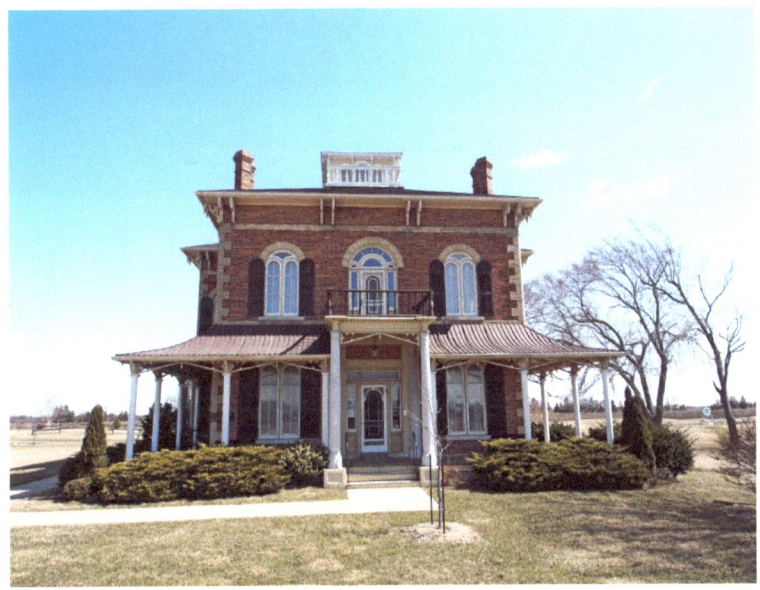

It is a 6,000 square foot home building. It has sixteen rooms, including five bedrooms, a music room and a widow's walk and rooftop belvedere.

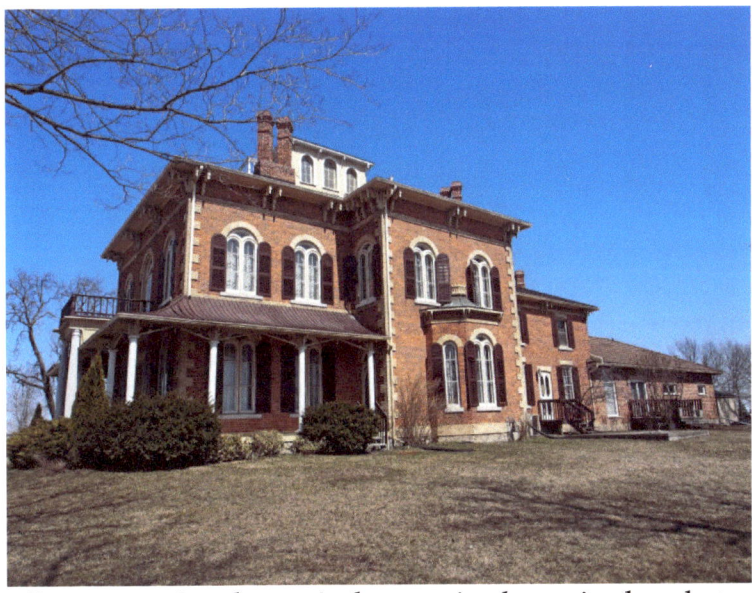

Corner quoins, bay window, paired cornice brackets

Building Styles

The **Farmhouse** is a country home style that highlights the simplicity of rural living. Comfort and function are the major themes that are associated with the style. The roof frequently flares out to cover the porch. The large porches were designed to help cool the interior of the home and also provide a shady spot for guests to gather and enjoy the outdoors. The architecture of a country home is minimally ornamental but very efficient with functional shutters, decorative porch railing, and dormer windows that increase interior light and living space. The exterior is typically faced with horizontal siding. Farmhouse floor plans are usually square or symmetrically shaped, sometimes with side wings. The interior has a large country kitchen and a cluster of bedrooms on the upper level. Farmhouses contain at least one fireplace and large family gathering areas designed for relaxation. The country home is casual, functional and comfortable. Well-crafted and sturdy, farmhouses are generally built to last and withstand for ages.

Gothic Revival, 1830-1890 – These decorative buildings have sharply-pitched gables with highly detailed verge boards, pointed-arch window openings, and dichromatic brickwork. It is a common style in Ontario.

Italianate, 1850-1900 – A two story rectangular building with a mild hip roof, a projecting frontispiece, and generous eaves with ornate cornice brackets was the basis of the style; often there are large sash windows, quoins, ornate detailing on the windows, belvederes and wraparound verandahs. Italianate commercial buildings often have cast iron cresting and elegant window surrounds.

A **log cabin**, built from logs, was usually one- or 1½-storys constructed with round rather than hewn, or hand-worked, logs, and erected quickly for frontier shelter. Log cabins were built from logs laid horizontally and interlocked on the ends with notches. The cabin was situated to provide sunlight and drainage so the pioneers could cope better with the rigors of frontier life. The pioneers chose old-growth trees that were straight and had few knots and did not need to be hewn to fit well together. Careful notching minimized the size of the gap between the logs and reduced the amount of chinking with sticks and rocks or daubing with mud to fill the gap. The length of one log was the length of one wall.

Romanesque Revival, 1880-1910 – This style hearkens back to medieval architecture of the 11th and 12th centuries with a heavy appearance, blocky towers and rounded arches.

Second Empire, 1860-1880 – The mansard roof is the most noteworthy feature of this style and is evidence of the French origins. Projecting central towers and one or two-story bays can also be present.

Other Books by Barbara Raue

Coins of Gold
Arrows, Indians and Love
The Life and Times of Barbara
The Cromwell Family Book
Laura Secord Discovered
Daddy Where Are You?

Montana Series
Book 1: Montana Dream
Book 2: Life on the Montana Frontier
Book 3: Montana to Boston and Back
Book 4: Montana Sons Go to War
Book 5: Montana Sons Return from War

Visit Barbara's website to view all of her books
http://barbararaue.ca

Other books on Haldimand County:
Cayuga and York Ontario in Colour Photos
Dunnville Ontario Book 1 in Colour Photos
Dunnville Ontario Book 2 and Other Haldimand County towns in Colour Photos
Hagersville Ontario in Colour Photos
Jarvis and Port Dover Ontario in Colour Photos

Barbara is The Authority on Saving Our History One Photo at a Time. She is pursuing her interest in photography and architecture by preserving a record through photos of old buildings from the 1800s and 1900s with their unique architecture. Enjoy the beautiful architecture in the comfort of your living room. Dream about what it was like in those by-gone days. Dream about what it was like to live in a mansion like one of those in this book.

Barbara Raue, a wife, mother and grandmother, is an avid reader and writer. She has researched and compiled several family histories. In 2010, Barbara published her book "Coins of Gold," which celebrates the courageous life of her mother, May Todd. Barbara's second book is a historical fiction "Arrows, Indians and Love" which takes place in Boonesborough, Kentucky during the time of Daniel Boone. In 2013, Barbara published *The Cromwell Family Book* in which she traces her ancestry generations back into Great Britain. Her second novel is called *Laura Secord Discovered,* in which the story of Laura's service during the War of 1812 is shared. Barbara's memoir is titled *Daddy Where Are You?* It tells of her life growing up without a father. Five novels in the Montana Series have been published, *Montana Dream, Life on the Montana Frontier, Montana to Boston and Back, Montana Sons Go to War*, and *Montana Sons Return from War*. The Donaldson series of two novels is available: *Rite of Passage* and *Rite of Marriage.*

This is a link to Barbara's website to view all of her books
http://barbararaue.ca

www.ingramcontent.com/pod-product-compliance
Lightning Source LLC
Chambersburg PA
CBHW040230220526
45473CB00001B/187